Grammar
Mate 2

저자 약력

이강희 (전) 한국 외국어대학교 외국어연수 평가원 영어 전임 강사
하와이 주립대 Second Language Studies 석사
한국 외국어대학교 영어과 학사
〈Grammar's Cool〉 (YBM), 〈빠르게 잡는 유형독해 Level 2〉 (천재교육)
〈New TOEIC 콩나물 Basic Listening〉 (두산동아), 〈TOEIC CLINIC Beginner〉 (위트앤위즈덤) 등 다수의 교재 공저

전지원 미국 오리건 주립대 Linguistics 석사
(현) 한국 외국어대학교 외국어연수 평가원 영어 전임 강사
〈내공 중학 영작문〉 (다락원), 〈Grammar plus Writing〉 (다락원), 〈Grammar plus Writing Start〉 (다락원),
〈Grammar's Cool〉 (YBM), 〈빠르게 잡는 영문법〉 (천재교육) 등 다수의 교재 공저

박혜영 미국 하와이 주립대 Second Language Studies 석사
(현) 한국 외국어대학교 외국어연수 평가원 영어 전임 강사
〈내공 중학 영작문〉 (다락원), 〈Grammar plus Writing〉 (다락원), 〈Grammar plus Writing Start〉 (다락원),
〈Grammar's Cool〉 (YBM), 〈빠르게 잡는 영문법〉 (천재교육) 등 다수의 교재 공저

Grammar Mate ②

지은이 이강희, 전지원, 박혜영

펴낸이 정규도
펴낸곳 (주)다락원

초판 1쇄 발행 2020년 2월 10일
초판 4쇄 발행 2023년 8월 25일

편집 서정아, 서민정, 김민아
디자인 구수정
삽화 김주연
영문 감수 Michael A. Putlack

다락원 경기도 파주시 문발로 211
내용문의 (02)736-2031 내선 503
구입문의 (02)736-2031 내선 250~252

Fax (02)732-2037
출판등록 1977년 9월 16일 제 406-2008-000007호

ISBN 978-89-277-0873-5 64740
978-89-277-0871-1 64740(set)

http://www.darakwon.co.kr
다락원 홈페이지를 방문하시면 상세한 출판정보와 함께
동영상강좌, MP3 자료 등 다양한 어학 정보를 얻으실 수 있습니다.

Grammar
Mate 2

DARAKWON

Introduction

Grammar Mate 시리즈는

Core basic English grammar

초급 학습자들에게 꼭 필요한 핵심 문법 사항을 수록하여 영문법의 기초를
탄탄히 다질 수 있도록 하였습니다.

Easy, clear explanations of grammar rules and concepts

문법 개념과 용어를 쉽고 명료하게 설명하였습니다. 포괄적인 문법 설명을 지양하고
세분화된 단원 구성과 포인트 별 핵심 설명으로 확실한 이해를 도울 수 있도록 하였습니다.

Plenty of various step–by-step exercises

다양하고 풍부한 연습 문제를 제공합니다. 지나친 drill이나 서술형 등 한쪽으로
치우친 유형이 아닌, 개념 이해부터 적용까지 체계적이고 다양한 문제 풀이를 통해
자연스럽게 문법 개념을 익힐 수 있습니다.

Writing exercises to develop writing skills and grammar accuracy

문법 학습 후 문장 쓰기 연습을 통해 내신 서술형에 대비할 수 있습니다.
또한 영어 문장을 써봄으로써 답을 맞추기 위한 문법이 아니라 영어라는 큰 틀 안에서
문법을 정확히 활용할 수 있도록 하였습니다.

Comprehensive tests to prepare for actual school tests

각 CHAPTER가 끝날 때마다 실제 학교 내신 시험에서 출제되는 문제 유형들로 구성된
테스트를 제공하여 학교 내신 시험에 익숙해질 수 있도록 하였습니다.

Workbook for further practice

워크북을 통한 추가 문제를 제공함으로써 문법 개념을 숙지할 때까지
충분한 문제와 복습 컨텐츠를 제공합니다.

How to Use This Book

GRAMMAR POINT

초급자가 알아야 할 문법 사항을 도표, 사진, 실용적인 예문을 통해 이해하기 쉽게 설명하였습니다.
주의해야 할 사항은 **NOTE** 로, 더 알아야 할 사항은 **+PLUS** 로 제시하였습니다.

LET'S CHECK

왼쪽 페이지에서 학습한 내용을 개념 확인 문제를 통해 바로 연습해볼 수 있습니다.

LET'S PRACTICE

보다 풍부한 연습 문제를 통해 문법 실력을 다질 수 있습니다.

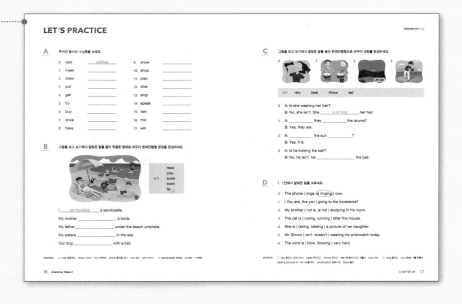

LET'S WRITE

문법 사항을 문장 쓰기에
적용해봄으로써 학습 효과를
증대시키고 내신 서술형에
대비할 수 있습니다.
빈칸 완성, 어구 배열, 영작하기
문제로 구성되어 있습니다.

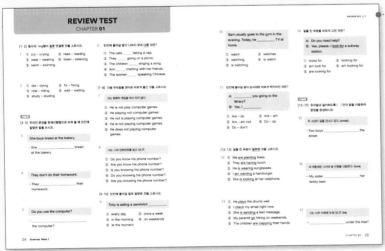

REVIEW TEST

각 CHAPTER가 끝날 때마다
학습한 문법 사항을 총 정리할
수 있고, 나아가 실제 내신 문제
유형에 익숙해질 수 있습니다.

WORKBOOK

워크북을 통해 학습한 해당
UNIT의 문법사항을 다시 한번
복습하며 실력을 점검해볼 수
있습니다.

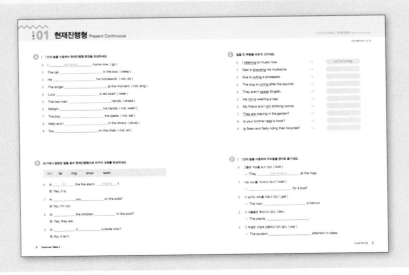

Contents

Grammar Mate 1 목차

Grammar Mate 3 목차

CHAPTER
01

Present Continuous
현재진행형

LET′S LOOK

She **is eating** pizza.

They **are moving** boxes.

현재진행형은 '~하고 있다, ~하는 중이다'의 의미로 지금 진행 중인 일을 나타낸다. 현재진행형은 「be동사의 현재형＋동사원형-ing」형태로 나타낸다.

UNIT 01 현재진행형
Present Continuous

1 현재진행형

❶ 현재진행형은 '~하고 있다, ~하는 중이다'의 의미로 지금 진행 중인 일을 나타낸다.

Ann **drinks** a cup of tea every morning.

Ann **is drinking** a cup of tea *now*.

❷ 현재진행형은 주어의 인칭과 수에 따라 「be동사의 현재형 + 동사원형-ing」 형태로 쓴다.

I	am	reading.
You/We/They	are	working.
He/She/It	is	sleeping.

> **NOTE** 1. 현재진행형은 now(지금), right now(바로 지금), at the moment(지금은) 등의 시간 표현과 함께 쓸 수 있다.
>
> I **am cooking** dinner *now*.　　She **is working** *at the moment*.
>
> 2. 현재진행형에서 「주어 + be동사」는 줄여 쓸 수 있다.
>
> I**'m eating** lunch.　　He**'s watching** a movie.　　They**'re singing** a song.

2 동사의 -ing형 만들기

대부분의 동사	+ -ing	go → go**ing**	play → play**ing**
-e로 끝나는 동사	e를 빼고 + -ing	come → com**ing**	write → writ**ing**
〈단모음 + 단자음〉으로 끝나는 동사	자음을 한번 더 쓰고 + -ing	sit → si**tting**　cut → cu**tting**　run → run**ning**　swim → swim**ming**	
-ie로 끝나는 동사	ie를 y로 고치고 + -ing	lie → l**ying**　die → d**ying**　tie → t**ying**	

The kids **are playing** in the garden.

I **am writing** an email right now.

She **is cutting** an apple with a knife.

The dog **is lying** on the grass.

> **NOTE** 1. 〈모음 2개 + 자음〉으로 끝나는 동사는 마지막 자음 추가 없이 -ing만 붙인다.
>
> rain → rain**ing**　　wait → wait**ing**　　beat → beat**ing**
>
> 2. w, x, y로 끝나는 동사는 -ing만 붙인다.
>
> snow → snow**ing**　　fix → fix**ing**　　study → study**ing**

LET'S CHECK

A

주어진 동사의 -ing형을 쓰세요.

0	go	_going_	10	eat	_____
1	take	_____	11	say	_____
2	read	_____	12	smile	_____
3	sit	_____	13	die	_____
4	watch	_____	14	cry	_____
5	lie	_____	15	ride	_____
6	cook	_____	16	sing	_____
7	sleep	_____	17	cut	_____
8	clean	_____	18	study	_____
9	write	_____	19	stop	_____

B

( ) 안의 말을 이용하여 현재진행형 문장을 완성하세요.

0   The boy _____is drinking_____ Coke. (drink)

1   Look! It _____ outside. (snow)

2   Hurry up! The bus _____. (come)

3   I _____ my homework right now. (do)

4   She _____ some flowers. (buy)

5   The kids _____ on the trampoline. (jump)

6   Dave _____ his shoe. (tie)

7   Jane _____ on her coat. (put)

8   Sam and I _____ table tennis. (play)

9   Some people _____ in the park. (run)

WORDS   A lie 눕다; 거짓말하다   die 죽다   ride 타다   B outside 밖에   trampoline 트램펄린   tie 묶다   put on ~을 입다   table tennis 탁구

3　현재진행형의 부정문

「be동사의 현재형 + not + 동사원형-ing」의 형태이며, '~하고 있지 않다'의 의미이다.

I	am		reading.
You/We/They	are	not	working.
He/She/It	is		sleeping.

> **NOTE**　현재진행형의 부정문에서 「주어 + be동사」 또는 「be동사 + not」은 줄여 쓸 수 있다.
> I **am not** running.　→　**I'm not** running.
> They **are not** fighting.　→　They**'re not** fighting. / They **aren't** fighting.
> He **is not** studying.　→　He**'s not** studying. / He **isn't** studying.

4　현재진행형의 의문문

「be동사의 현재형 + 주어 + 동사원형-ing?」의 형태이며, '~하고 있니?'의 의미이다.

의문문			긍정의 대답	부정의 대답
Am	I	reading?	Yes, 주어 + am/are/is.	No, 주어 + 'm not/aren't/isn't.
Are	you/we/they	working?		
Is	he/she/it	sleeping?		

A: **Am I talking** too loudly?
B: **Yes, you are. / No, you aren't.**

A: **Are you reading** a book? 〈you = 단수(너, 당신)〉
B: **Yes, I am. / No, I'm not.**

A: **Are you enjoying** the party? 〈you = 복수(너희들, 여러분)〉
B: **Yes, we are. / No, we aren't.**

A: **Is the panda sleeping?**
B: **Yes, it is. / No, it isn't.**

LET'S CHECK

C　( ) 안의 말을 이용하여 현재진행형 부정문을 완성하세요.

0　It _____isn't raining_____ outside. It is sunny. (rain)

1　The baby _____ . He is smiling. (cry)

2　The girls _____ . They are singing. (dance)

3　I _____ to music. I am watching TV. (listen)

4　The teacher _____ . He is standing. (sit)

5　The cat _____ . It is yawning. (sleep)

6　Mike _____ . He is walking. (run)

7　The students _____ . They are playing. (study)

8　James _____ a hat today. (wear)

9　My mother _____ in the kitchen. (cook)

D　( ) 안의 말을 이용하여 현재진행형 의문문을 완성하세요.

0　_____Is_____ Mr. Kim ___teaching___ his class? (teach)

1　_____ you _____ a cake? (make)

2　_____ they _____ their vacation? (enjoy)

3　_____ Tom and Sue _____ to the zoo? (go)

4　_____ John _____ his mother? (help)

5　_____ the men _____ in the sea? (swim)

6　_____ the children _____? (laugh)

7　_____ I _____ you? (bother)

8　_____ the boy _____ a kite? (fly)

9　_____ they _____ to us? (wave)

WORDS　**C** stand 서다, 서 있다　yawn 하품하다　hat 모자　**D** vacation 휴가, 방학　laugh 웃다　bother 귀찮게 하다, 성가시게 하다
fly a kite 연을 날리다　wave 손을 흔들다

LET'S PRACTICE

A 주어진 동사의 -ing형을 쓰세요.

0	visit	_visiting_	9	snow	_____
1	meet	_____	10	shop	_____
2	draw	_____	11	plan	_____
3	put	_____	12	dive	_____
4	get	_____	13	stop	_____
5	try	_____	14	speak	_____
6	buy	_____	15	rain	_____
7	drive	_____	16	mix	_____
8	have	_____	17	win	_____

B 그림을 보고 보기에서 알맞은 말을 골라 적절한 형태로 바꾸어 현재진행형 문장을 완성하세요.

보기	read play ~~build~~ swim lie

I ____am building____ a sandcastle.

My mother _____ a book.

My father _____ under the beach umbrella.

My sisters _____ in the sea.

Our dog _____ with a ball.

WORDS A visit 방문하다 draw 그리다 try 노력하다 shop 물건을 사다 mix 섞다 win 이기다 B sandcastle 모래성 under ~ 아래에

C

그림을 보고 보기에서 알맞은 말을 골라 현재진행형으로 바꾸어 대화를 완성하세요.

0  1  2  3

보기   ~~dry~~   beat   throw   set

0 A: Is she washing her hair?

B: No, she isn't. She _____ is drying _____ her hair.

1 A: _____ they _____ the drums?

B: Yes, they are.

2 A: _____ the sun _____ ?

B: Yes, it is.

3 A: Is he kicking the ball?

B: No, he isn't. He _____ the ball.

D

( ) 안에서 알맞은 말을 고르세요.

0 The phone (rings, (is ringing)) now.

1 (You are, Are you) going to the bookstore?

2 My brother (not is, is not) studying in his room.

3 The cat is (runing, running) after the mouse.

4 She is (taking, takeing) a picture of her daughter.

5 Mr. Brown (isn't, doesn't) wearing his wristwatch today.

6 The wind is (blow, blowing) very hard.

WORDS   C dry 말리다, 건조시키다   beat 두드리다   throw 던지다   set (해·달이) 지다, 저물다   kick 차다   D ring 울리다   run after ~를 뒤쫓다
take a picture of ~의 사진을 찍다   wristwatch 손목시계   blow 불다

현재시제 vs. 현재진행형
Present Simple vs. Present Continuous

1 현재시제와 현재진행형

❶ 일반동사의 현재형은 현재의 사실, 반복적인 습관, 변함없는 진리를 나타낸다. 주어가 I/you/we/they일 때는 동사원형을 쓰고, 3인칭 단수(he/she/it)일 때는 동사원형에 주로 -(e)s를 붙인다.

긍정문	부정문	의문문
I **work**.	I **don't work**.	**Do** I **work**?
He **works**.	He **doesn't work**.	**Does** he **work**?
They **work**.	They **don't work**.	**Do** they **work**?

❷ 현재진행형은 지금 진행 중인 일을 나타낸다. 주어의 인칭과 수에 따라 「be동사의 현재형 + 동사원형-ing」 형태로 쓴다.

긍정문	부정문	의문문
I **am working**.	I**'m not working**.	**Am** I **working**?
He **is working**.	He **isn't working**.	**Is** he **working**?
They **are working**.	They **aren't working**.	**Are** they **working**?

> **NOTE**　1. 현재시제와 어울리는 표현: every day(매일), always(항상), usually(보통), often(가끔), sometimes(종종), rarely(거의 ~않다), never(결코 ~않다), once a week(일주일에 한 번), on Sundays(일요일마다) 등
>
> 　　2. 현재진행형과 어울리는 표현: now(지금), right now(바로 지금), at the moment(지금은) 등

2 진행형으로 쓸 수 없는 동사

❶ 감정, 소유, 생각 등 상태를 나타내는 동사는 현재진행형을 쓰지 않고 현재시제로 쓴다.

love	want	have	know	remember
like	need	own	understand	forget

I **am having** a pen. [×]	→	I **have** a pen. [○]
He **isn't knowing** my name. [×]	→	He **doesn't know** my name. [○]
Are you **wanting** a sandwich? [×]	→	**Do** you **want** a sandwich? [○]

❷ have가 소유(가지다)의 뜻이 아닌 경우에는 진행형을 쓸 수 있다.

I **am having** lunch. 나는 점심 식사를 하고 있다.

They **are having** a good time. 그들은 즐거운 시간을 보내고 있다.

LET'S CHECK

A 주어진 동사의 현재형 또는 현재진행형을 써서 문장을 완성하세요.

0   drink   (1) I _____drink_____ milk every morning.

                  (2) I _____am drinking_____ milk now.

1   go   (1) Sally _____ shopping on weekends.

             (2) Sally _____ shopping now.

2   feed   (1) I _____ my dog twice a day.

               (2) I _____ my dog right now.

3   help   (1) My sister and I often _____ our mother.

               (2) We _____ our mother right now.

4   wear   (1) Bob usually _____ a suit.

                (2) Today, he _____ jeans and a T-shirt.

B ( ) 안에서 알맞은 말을 고르세요.

0   Judy (reads, (is reading)) a magazine right now.

1   I (need, am needing) a battery for my clock.

2   Lisa (drinks, is drinking) lemonade now.

3   (Do you know, Are you knowing) their names?

4   My brother (doesn't like, isn't liking) broccoli.

5   The girl (practices, is practicing) the flute right now.

6   I'm thirsty. I (want, am wanting) a glass of water.

7   Rick (has, is having) books in his bag.

8   The children (have, are having) their lunch at the moment.

WORDS   **A** feed 먹이를 주다   suit 정장   jeans 청바지   **B** magazine 잡지   practice 연습하다   flute 플루트   thirsty 목마른

LET'S PRACTICE

 A 보기에서 알맞은 말을 골라 문장을 완성하세요. (단, 한 번씩만 쓸 것)

보기	~~usually~~	on Fridays	at the moment

0   I _____usually_____ have toast and eggs for breakfast.

1   Emily is making her bed _____.

2   Mike takes a bowling class _____.

보기	right now	once a month	today

3   They go to the movies _____.

4   Sarah is washing her hands _____.

5   Chris isn't wearing glasses _____.

B ( ) 안에서 알맞은 말을 고르세요.

0   (Are, (Do)) you like dinosaurs?

1   The bus (isn't, doesn't) moving right now.

2   (Is, Does) she crying or laughing?

3   I (am not, don't) understand this question.

4   Andy, you (aren't, don't) wearing your seatbelt.

5   Sadly, she (isn't, doesn't) know the truth.

6   Ryan (isn't, doesn't) studying English now.

7   (Are, Do) they having a good time?

8   Nick (is, does) eating a sandwich in the cafeteria.

9   Excuse me. (Am, Do) I know you?

WORDS   **A** toast 토스트   make one's bed 침대를 정리하다   glasses 안경   **B** dinosaur 공룡   understand 이해하다   seatbelt 안전벨트   truth 진실   cafeteria 카페테리아, 구내식당

C ( ) 안의 말을 이용하여 현재형 또는 현재진행형 문장을 완성하세요.

0 The moon _____goes_____ around the Earth. (go)

1 Shh. The baby _____. (sleep)

2 The girls _____ rope now. (jump)

3 Bill likes sports. He often _____ tennis. (play)

4 We _____ breakfast in the morning. (eat)

5 It _____! Let's make a snowman. (snow)

6 Ann never eats meat. She _____ it. (not, like)

7 He is a liar. I _____ him. (not, believe)

8 The elevator _____ at the moment. (not, work)

9 Molly _____ late on Sundays. (get up)

D 밑줄 친 부분을 바르게 고치세요.

0 Jason is having a sister. → has

1 Are you believing in UFOs? →

2 The baby drinks milk now. →

3 Julie is liking her black jacket. →

4 This tea is good. I'm loving it. →

5 Dad is washes his car at the moment. →

6 Listen! Someone knocks on the door. →

7 The club members are meeting on Tuesdays. →

8 He not is reading a book right now. →

9 Do you watching that TV show? →

WORDS　C jump rope 줄넘기를 하다　meat 고기　liar 거짓말쟁이　work 일하다; *작동하다　D believe in (~의 존재를) 믿다
knock 두드리다, 노크하다

STEP 1 빈칸 완성 보기에서 알맞은 말을 골라 적절한 형태로 바꾸어 문장을 완성하세요.

보기	read	fix	do	sit	pour

1   그들은 버스에 앉아 있다.

→ They _____ _____ on the bus.

2   그 남자는 차를 고치고 있다.

→ The man _____ _____ a car.

3   나는 지금 숙제를 하고 있지 않다.

→ I _____ _____ _____ my homework now.

4   그녀는 컵에 물을 따르고 있다.

→ She _____ _____ water into a cup.

5   너는 소설을 읽고 있니?

→ _____ _____ _____ a novel?

STEP 2 어구 배열 우리말과 일치하도록 ( ) 안의 말을 알맞게 배열하세요.

6   나는 창밖을 내다보고 있다. (the, I, looking out, am, window)

→ _____

7   Sally는 인터넷으로 쇼핑을 하고 있다. (Sally, shopping, is, on the Internet)

→ _____

8   Tom은 그의 방을 청소하고 있지 않다. (Tom, his, not, is, cleaning, room)

→ _____

9   Jessica는 지금 통화 중이니? (Jessica, talking, is, on the phone)

→ _____ now?

10   초인종이 울리고 있니? (doorbell, ringing, is, the)

→ _____

STEP 3

영작하기 (   ) 안의 말을 이용하여 우리말을 영어로 옮기세요.

11 우리는 해변을 걷고 있다. (walk, on the beach)

→ _____

12 그들은 천장에 페인트를 칠하고 있다. (paint, the ceiling)

→ _____

13 그녀는 손톱을 자르고 있다. (cut, her fingernails)

→ _____

14 사람들은 잔디 위에 누워있다. (lie, on the grass)

→ _____

15 너는 진실을 말하고 있지 않다. (tell, the truth)

→ _____

16 그들은 식당에서 식사를 하고 있지 않다. (eat, at a restaurant)

→ _____

17 그는 오늘 넥타이를 매고 있지 않다. (wear, a tie)

→ _____ today.

18 물이 끓고 있니? (the water, boil)

→ _____

19 내가 너무 빨리 걷고 있니? (walk, too fast)

→ _____

20 저에게 질문하시는 건가요? (ask, me)

→ _____

REVIEW TEST
CHAPTER 01

[1-2] 동사의 -ing형이 잘못 연결된 것을 고르시오.

1 ① cry – crying   ② read – reading
     ③ wear – wearing   ④ listen – listening
     ⑤ swim – swiming

2 ① die – dying   ② fix – fixing
     ③ ride – riding   ④ wait – waiting
     ⑤ study – studing

서술형

[3-5] 다음 문장을 현재진행형으로 바꿔 쓸 때 빈칸에
알맞은 말을 쓰시오.

3
She buys bread at the bakery.

→ She _____ _____ bread
at the bakery.

4
They don't do their homework.

→ They _____ _____ their
homework.

5
Do you use the computer?

→ _____ _____ _____
the computer?

6 빈칸에 들어갈 말이 나머지 넷과 다른 것은?

     ① The cats _____ taking a nap.
     ② They _____ going on a picnic.
     ③ The children _____ singing a song.
     ④ Ann _____ chatting with her friends.
     ⑤ The women _____ speaking Chinese.

[7-8] 다음 우리말을 영어로 바르게 옮긴 것을 고르시오.

7
그는 컴퓨터 게임을 하고 있지 않다.

     ① He is not play computer games.
     ② He playing not computer games.
     ③ He not is playing computer games.
     ④ He is not playing computer games.
     ⑤ He does not playing computer games.

8
너는 그의 전화번호를 알고 있니?

     ① Do you know his phone number?
     ② Are you know his phone number?
     ③ Is you knowing his phone number?
     ④ Do you knowing his phone number?
     ⑤ Are you knowing his phone number?

[9-10] 빈칸에 들어갈 말로 알맞은 것을 고르시오.

9
Tony is eating a sandwich _____.

     ① every day   ② once a week
     ③ in the morning   ④ on weekends
     ⑤ at the moment

10
Sam usually goes to the gym in the evening. Today, he _____ TV at home.

① watch   ② watches
③ watching   ④ is watch
⑤ is watching

11 빈칸에 들어갈 말이 순서대로 바르게 짝지어진 것은?

A: _____ you going to the library?
B: Yes, I _____.

① Are – do   ② Are – am
③ Are – am not   ④ Do – do
⑤ Do – don't

[12-13] 밑줄 친 부분이 잘못된 것을 고르시오.

12 ① We are planting trees.
② They are having lunch.
③ He is wearing sunglasses.
④ I am wanting a hamburger.
⑤ She is looking at her cellphone.

13 ① He plays the drums well.
② I check my email right now.
③ She is sending a text message.
④ My parents go hiking on weekends.
⑤ The children are clapping their hands.

14 밑줄 친 부분을 바르게 고친 것은?

A: Do you need help?
B: Yes, please. I look for a subway station.

① looks for   ② looking for
③ am look for   ④ am looking for
⑤ are looking for

서술형

[15-17] 우리말과 일치하도록 ( ) 안의 말을 이용하여 문장을 완성하시오.

15
두 소년이 길을 건너고 있다. (cross)

→ Two boys _____ the street.

16
내 여동생은 그녀의 곰 인형을 사랑한다. (love)

→ My sister _____ her teddy bear.

17
그는 나무 아래에 누워 있니? (lie)

→ _____ under the tree?

CHAPTER
02

Past Simple
과거시제

LET'S LOOK

I **was** happy last Christmas.

It **snowed** a lot yesterday.

과거시제는 과거의 상태나 동작을 나타낸다. be동사의 과거형은 **was**, **were**를 쓰고 일반동사의 과거형은 동사원형에 주로 **-(e)d**를 붙여 만든다.

03 Be동사의 과거형
Past Simple: *Be*

1 be동사의 과거형

'~이었다, (~에) 있었다'라고 과거의 일을 말할 때는 be동사의 과거형 was, were를 사용한다.

I **am** 14 years old now.
I **was** 13 years old *last year*.

The kids **are** at home today.
They **were** at the zoo *yesterday*.

> **NOTE** 과거시제는 주로 yesterday(어제), last ~(지난 ~), ~ ago(~ 전에), in 2017(2017년에), then(그때) 등 과거를 나타내는 시간 표현과 함께 쓰인다.

2 be동사 과거형의 긍정문과 부정문

am, is의 과거형은 was를, are의 과거형은 were를 쓴다. 부정문은 「was/were + not」의 형태이며, '~이 아니었다, (~에) 없었다'의 의미이다.

긍정문		부정문	
I/He/She/It	was	I/He/She/It	was not (= wasn't)
You/We/They	were	You/We/They	were not (= weren't)

The class **was** boring yesterday. It **wasn't** interesting.
We **were** at the mall an hour ago. We **weren't** at home.

3 be동사 과거형의 의문문

「Was/Were + 주어 ~?」의 형태이며, '~이었니?, (~에) 있었니?'의 의미이다.

의문문	긍정의 대답	부정의 대답
Was + 주어 ~?	Yes, 주어 + was.	No, 주어 + wasn't.
Were + 주어 ~?	Yes, 주어 + were.	No, 주어 + weren't.

A: **Was Tom** late for school yesterday?
B: **Yes, he was. / No, he wasn't.**

A: **Were you** at Silvia's birthday party last night?
B: **Yes, I was. / No, I wasn't.**

LET'S CHECK

A

( ) 안에서 알맞은 말을 고르세요.

0   He ((was), were) in his office.

1   The movie (wasn't, weren't) very scary.

2   I (wasn't, weren't) hungry this morning.

3   You (was, were) a very cute baby.

4   His advice (was, were) helpful.

5   It (was, were) a holiday yesterday.

6   They (was, were) in Canada in 2018.

7   The girls (was, were) in the cafeteria at lunchtime.

8   He and I (wasn't, weren't) close friends last year.

9   My brother (wasn't, weren't) tall a few years ago.

B

be동사를 이용하여 과거형 의문문과 대답을 완성하세요.

0   A: _____Were_____ you born in Korea?   B: Yes, _____I was_____.

1   A: _____ your father a teacher?   B: Yes, _____.

2   A: _____ the soccer game exciting?   B: No, _____.

3   A: _____ they in Spain last summer?   B: No, _____.

4   A: _____ the boxes heavy?   B: Yes, _____.

5   A: _____ it hot yesterday?   B: No, _____.

6   A: _____ he late again?   B: Yes, _____.

7   A: _____ you a good swimmer?   B: No, _____.

8   A: _____ the hotel expensive?   B: Yes, _____.

WORDS   **A** scary 무서운   advice 조언, 충고   helpful 도움이 되는   close 가까운; *친한   **B** exciting 신나는, 흥미진진한   heavy 무거운   expensive 비싼

LET'S PRACTICE

A ( ) 안에서 알맞은 말을 고르세요.

0   I (am, (was)) at school yesterday.

1   Look. The girl over there (is, was) my sister.

2   She (is, was) a nurse two years ago.

3   Laura (is, was) my classmate last year.

4   The music (is, was) too loud. Please turn it down.

5   Many years ago, there (is, was) a big pond here.

6   Seoul (is, was) the capital of Korea.

7   My cats (are, were) tiny a few months ago.

8   Daniel (is, was) late for work yesterday. The traffic (is, was) heavy.

9   The twins (are, were) born last year. They (are, were) 2 years old now.

B 그림을 보고 보기에서 알맞은 말을 골라 문장을 완성하세요. (중복 가능)

| 보기 | was | were | wasn't | weren't |

0   It _____was_____ rainy yesterday. It _____wasn't_____ sunny.

1   The exam _____ difficult. It _____ easy.

2   They _____ at home last week. They _____ on vacation.

3   Sally _____ a news reporter. She _____ a doctor.

WORDS   A nurse 간호사   turn down (소리 등을) 낮추다, 줄이다   pond 연못   capital 수도   tiny 아주 작은   twin 쌍둥이   B rainy 비가 오는   on vacation 휴가 중인   reporter 기자

C ( ) 안의 말과 be동사를 이용하여 과거형 문장을 쓰세요.

0 (my favorite toy / a teddy bear)

→ _____ My favorite toy was a teddy bear. _____

1 (Alex / born / in London)

→ _____

2 (This song / not / popular)

→ _____

3 (the trees / not / tall)

→ _____

4 (there / some books / on the desk)

→ _____

D ( ) 안의 말과 be동사를 이용하여 과거형 의문문과 대답을 완성하세요.

0 A: _____ Were you _____ sick yesterday? (you)

B: No, _____ I wasn't _____.

1 A: _____ at the gym this morning? (he)

B: Yes, _____.

2 A: _____ your neighbors? (they)

B: Yes, _____.

3 A: _____ here an hour ago? (Bill and Sue)

B: No, _____.

4 A: _____ cold last night? (it)

B: Yes, _____.

WORDS C popular 인기 있는 neighbor 이웃

04 일반동사의 과거형 1
Past Simple 1

1 일반동사의 과거형

❶ 일반동사의 과거형은 이미 끝나버린 과거의 상태나 동작을 나타낸다.

I **live** in Seoul now.
I **lived** in Seattle *last year*.

He usually **walks** to school.
He **walked** to school *yesterday*.

They **play** soccer once a week.
They **played** soccer *an hour ago*.

❷ 역사적 사실을 말할 때도 과거형을 쓴다.

King Sejong **created** Hanguel.
Christopher Columbus **arrived** in America in 1492.

2 일반동사 과거형의 형태

❶ 규칙 변화: 대부분 동사원형에 -(e)d를 붙여 과거형을 만든다.

대부분의 동사	+ -ed	help → help**ed** walk → walk**ed**
-e로 끝나는 동사	+ -d	arrive → arrive**d** close → close**d**
〈자음 + y〉로 끝나는 동사	y를 i로 고치고 + -ed	study → stud**ied** try → tr**ied** 〈모음 + y〉는 + -ed: play**ed**, enjoy**ed**, stay**ed**
〈단모음 + 단자음〉으로 끝나는 동사	자음을 한번 더 쓰고 + -ed	drop → drop**ped** hug → hug**ged** plan → plan**ned** stop → stop**ped**

Tom **helped** us yesterday.
She **closed** the door quietly.
We **studied** for the exam last week.
The car **stopped** at the traffic light.

LET'S CHECK

A 주어진 동사의 과거형을 쓰세요.

0	walk	walked	10	carry	_____
1	jump	_____	11	play	_____
2	finish	_____	12	stay	_____
3	laugh	_____	13	enjoy	_____
4	watch	_____	14	stop	_____
5	like	_____	15	drop	_____
6	dance	_____	16	plan	_____
7	smile	_____	17	pass	_____
8	cry	_____	18	want	_____
9	try	_____	19	shout	_____

B 주어진 동사의 현재형 또는 과거형을 써서 문장을 완성하세요.

0 live

(1) Eva ___lived___ in Japan two years ago.

(2) She ___lives___ in China now.

1 rain

(1) In my country, it _____ a lot in summer.

(2) It _____ a lot last summer.

2 study

(1) I _____ English every day.

(2) I _____ math yesterday.

3 arrive

(1) Paul usually _____ at school early.

(2) He _____ at school late this morning.

4 visit

(1) We _____ our grandparents every month.

(2) Last month, our grandparents _____ us.

WORDS A carry 운반하다 drop 떨어뜨리다 pass 합격하다; 지나가다 shout 소리치다 B arrive 도착하다

❷ 불규칙 변화

	현재	과거	현재	과거
현재형과 과거형의 형태가 같은 동사	cut (자르다)	cut	put (놓다, 두다)	put
	hit (치다)	hit	read [ri:d] (읽다)	read [réd]
현재형과 과거형의 형태가 다른 동사	become (되다)	became	make (만들다)	made
	break (깨다)	broke	meet (만나다)	met
	build (짓다)	built	ride (타다)	rode
	buy (사다)	bought	ring (소리가 울리다)	rang
	catch (잡다)	caught	rise (뜨다; 올리다)	rose
	come (오다)	came	run (달리다)	ran
	do (하다)	did	see (보다)	saw
	drink (마시다)	drank	sell (팔다)	sold
	drive (운전하다)	drove	send (보내다)	sent
	eat (먹다)	ate	sing (노래하다)	sang
	fall (떨어지다)	fell	sit (앉다)	sat
	feel (느끼다)	felt	sleep (자다)	slept
	find (발견하다)	found	spend (소비하다)	spent
	get (얻다)	got	swim (수영하다)	swam
	give (주다)	gave	take (잡다)	took
	go (가다)	went	teach (가르치다)	taught
	have (가지다)	had	tell (말하다)	told
	hear (듣다)	heard	wake (깨다)	woke
	know (알다)	knew	wear (입다)	wore
	leave (떠나다)	left	win (이기다)	won
	lose (잃다; 지다)	lost	write (쓰다)	wrote

The hairdresser **cut** my hair.

I **ate** dinner at 7 o'clock.

We **met** at a nice café yesterday.

My dog **slept** in my bed last night.

✏ NOTE read의 과거형은 현재형과 형태는 같지만 [réd]로 읽는다.

I **read** a book every day.
[ri:d]

I **read** an interesting book yesterday.
[réd]

LET'S CHECK

C
주어진 동사의 과거형을 쓰세요.

0	come	_came_	10	write	_____
1	do	_____	11	buy	_____
2	eat	_____	12	catch	_____
3	get	_____	13	drink	_____
4	go	_____	14	drive	_____
5	have	_____	15	read	_____
6	put	_____	16	ride	_____
7	see	_____	17	run	_____
8	sit	_____	18	teach	_____
9	sleep	_____	19	break	_____

D
주어진 동사의 현재형을 쓰세요.

0	heard	_hear_	10	cut	_____
1	left	_____	11	fell	_____
2	met	_____	12	hit	_____
3	rang	_____	13	knew	_____
4	sent	_____	14	built	_____
5	sang	_____	15	made	_____
6	took	_____	16	sold	_____
7	felt	_____	17	swam	_____
8	worn	_____	18	lost	_____
9	became	_____	19	won	_____

LET'S PRACTICE

A ( ) 안에서 알맞은 말을 고르세요.

0   I (take, (took)) a shower an hour ago.

1   Mary (got, gets) up early every morning.

2   The sun (rises, rose) at 6:18 this morning.

3   Julie and Tom (study, studied) together twice a week.

4   They (feel, felt) tired after the final exam.

5   He (writes, wrote) the novel in 1999.

6   Dad (cooks, cooked) spaghetti for us. It was delicious.

7   She listens to classical music (every day, yesterday).

8   Mr. and Mrs. Hill stayed at home (now, last night).

9   The department store closes at 9:00 p.m. (on Sundays, last Sunday).

B 주어진 문장을 과거형으로 바꿔 쓰세요.

0   I go skiing in winter.
     → _____ I went skiing _____ last week.

1   Janet wears a lovely hat.
     → _____ yesterday.

2   My mother drives me to school every day.
     → _____ this morning.

3   My uncle has two dogs.
     → _____ two years ago.

4   The train leaves every 30 minutes.
     → _____ 10 minutes ago.

WORDS   A tired 피곤한   novel 소설   delicious 맛있는   department store 백화점   B go skiing 스키 타러 가다   leave 떠나다, 출발하다

C ( ) 안의 말을 이용하여 과거형 문장을 완성하세요.

0   He _____ate_____ too much last night. (eat)

1   Our team _____ the game. (win)

2   We _____ in the sea yesterday. (swim)

3   My brother _____ the vase on the floor. (drop)

4   The model _____ his clothes quickly. (change)

5   She _____ an actress at the age of 20. (become)

6   My father _____ a new car last month. (buy)

7   The boy _____ off the bike and _____. (fall, cry)

D 그림을 보고 보기에서 알맞은 동사를 골라 적절한 형태로 바꾸어 문장을 완성하세요. (단, 한 번씩만 쓸 것)

보기	catch	run
	call	see
	~~go~~	shout
	hear	walk

Last night, Mr. and Mrs. Smith _____went_____ to bed early. At midnight, they

_____ a noise downstairs. Mr. Smith _____ downstairs and

_____ a thief. He _____, and the thief _____ away. Mrs.

Smith _____ the police. Fortunately, the police _____ the thief after a

few hours. It was a terrible night.

WORDS   C vase 꽃병   floor 바닥   change one's cloths 옷을 갈아입다   actress 여배우   fall off ~에서 떨어지다   D midnight 자정
downstairs 아래층에서[으로]   thief 도둑   run away 도망치다, 달아나다   fortunately 다행스럽게도   terrible 끔찍한

05 일반동사의 과거형 2
Past Simple 2

1

일반동사 과거형의 부정문

주어의 인칭과 수에 관계없이 「did not + 동사원형」의 형태이며, '~하지 않았다'의 의미이다.

주어	did not (= didn't)	동사원형

I **watched** TV last night.

→ I **didn't watch** TV last night.

She **ate** breakfast this morning.

→ She **didn't eat** breakfast this morning.

2

일반동사 과거형의 의문문

주어의 인칭과 수에 관계없이 「Did + 주어 + 동사원형?」의 형태이며, '~했니?'의 의미이다.

의문문			긍정의 대답	부정의 대답
Did	주어	동사원형?	Yes, 주어 + did.	No, 주어 + didn't.

A: **Did you like** the movie?

B: **Yes, I did. / No, I didn't.**

A: **Did Peter run** to school this morning?

B: **Yes, he did. / No, he didn't.**

A: **Did the kids make** this snowman?

B: **Yes, they did. / No, they didn't.**

 NOTE 일반동사의 부정문과 의문문을 만들 때 사용하는 did는 조동사이다. 일반동사 do(하다)의 과거형인 did와 혼동하지 않도록 주의하자.

Tom *did* his homework last night. → Tom **didn't** *do* his homework last night.

Did Tom *do* his homework last night?

LET'S CHECK

A 주어진 문장을 부정문으로 바꿔 쓰세요. (줄임말을 쓸 것)

0   Tom cleaned his room yesterday.

→ Tom _____didn't clean_____ his room yesterday.

1   We went to the aquarium last Sunday.

→ We _____ to the aquarium last Sunday.

2   They finished their work yesterday.

→ They _____ their work yesterday.

3   Everyone liked the idea.

→ Everyone _____ the idea.

4   The alarm clock rang this morning.

→ The alarm clock _____ this morning.

B ( ) 안의 말을 이용하여 과거형 의문문을 완성하세요.

0   A: _____Did_____ Ann _____draw_____ this picture? (draw)

B: Yes, she did.

1   A: _____ Mr. Kim _____ your class last year? (teach)

B: No, he didn't.

2   A: _____ Paul and Julie _____ the exam? (pass)

B: Yes, they did.

3   A: _____ you _____ your key? (find)

B: No, I didn't.

4   A: _____ you _____ to the park yesterday? (go)

B: Yes, we did.

WORDS   **A** aquarium 수족관   **B** alarm clock 자명종

LET'S PRACTICE

 A   ( ) 안에서 알맞은 말을 고르세요.

0   Rosa was tired. She (go, (went)) to bed early.

1   The musical was great. Everyone (enjoys, enjoyed) it.

2   Sorry. I (didn't, wasn't) understand your question.

3   David left work early. He didn't (feel, felt) well.

4   He was thirsty. He (drinked, drank) four glasses of water.

5   I (don't, didn't) break the glass. My brother did it.

6   The class was boring. I (fall, fell) asleep in class.

7   Sally (has, had) a bad cold last week.

8   I (don't, didn't) buy that shirt. It was too expensive.

B   주어진 문장을 부정문과 의문문으로 바꿔 쓰세요. (줄임말을 쓸 것)

0   Rick invited you to the party.

(1) 부정문: _____ Rick didn't invite you to the party. _____

(2) 의문문: _____ Did Rick invite you to the party? _____

1   She lost her car key yesterday.

(1) 부정문: _____

(2) 의문문: _____

2   They moved to a new house.

(1) 부정문: _____

(2) 의문문: _____

3   The school bus arrived on time.

(1) 부정문: _____

(2) 의문문: _____

WORDS   A musical 뮤지컬 question 질문 glass (유리) 잔 boring 지루한 fall asleep 잠들다   B invite 초대하다 on time 제시간에

C 그림을 보고 ( ) 안의 말을 이용하여 과거형 의문문과 대답을 완성하세요.

0

A: _____Did_____ Jane _____cry_____ during the movie? (cry)

B: Yes, _____she did_____.

1

A: _____ Mike _____ his arm? (break)

B: Yes, _____.

2

A: _____ you _____ to school? (walk)

B: No, _____.

3

A: _____ the shop _____ yesterday? (open)

B: No, _____.

D 밑줄 친 부분을 바르게 고치세요.

0 We <u>don't</u> play tennis last week. → *didn't*

1 My mom didn't <u>liked</u> cats. →

2 <u>Do</u> you see the rainbow this morning? →

3 <u>Was</u> the accident happen yesterday? →

4 Did Eva and Justin <u>got</u> married in 2015? →

5 A: Did he close the window? →
    B: No, he <u>did</u>.

WORDS D rainbow 무지개 accident 사고 happen 일어나다, 발생하다 get married 결혼하다

빈칸 완성 빈칸에 알맞은 be동사를 넣어 문장을 완성하세요.

1 그는 농구 선수였다.

→ He _____ a basketball player.

2 우리는 그때 공항에 있었다.

→ We _____ at the airport at that time.

3 나는 수학을 잘 못했다.

→ I _____ good at math.

4 Tom과 Bill은 배가 고프지 않았다.

→ Tom and Bill _____ hungry.

5 너는 오늘 아침에 바빴니?

→ _____ you busy this morning?

어구 배열 우리말과 일치하도록 ( ) 안의 말을 알맞게 배열하세요.

6 그녀는 지난 달에 새 차를 샀다. (she, new, bought, a, car)

→ _____ last month.

7 그들의 아들은 배우가 되었다. (their, actor, became, an, son)

→ _____

8 너는 택시를 타고 집에 왔니? (you, come, did, home, by taxi)

→ _____

9 우리는 어제 그를 만나지 않았다. (we, meet, didn't, him)

→ _____ yesterday.

10 Paul이 이 사진들을 찍었니? (take, Paul, these, did, pictures)

→ _____

STEP 3

영작하기 (   ) 안의 말을 이용하여 우리말을 영어로 옮기세요.

11 우리는 작년에 6학년이었다. (in the sixth grade, last year)

→ _____

12 우리는 지난 주말에 캠핑을 갔다. (go camping, last weekend)

→ _____

13 그녀는 그 케이크를 반으로 잘랐다. (cut, the cake, in half)

→ _____

14 그들은 점심 식사 후에 차를 마셨다. (drink, tea, after lunch)

→ _____

15 어제는 날씨가 좋지 않았다. (the weather, good, yesterday)

→ _____

16 그녀는 내 메시지를 읽지 않았다. (read, my message)

→ _____

17 우리는 그 호텔에 묵지 않았다. (stay, at the hotel)

→ _____

18 그녀는 어제 학교에 늦었니? (late for school, yesterday)

→ _____

19 너는 지난 밤에 잘 잤니? (sleep well, last night)

→ _____

20 너는 어제 그 가수를 보았니? (see, the singer, yesterday)

→ _____

REVIEW TEST
CHAPTER 02

[1-2] 동사의 현재형과 과거형이 잘못 연결된 것을 고르시오.

1
① cry – cried   ② read – read
③ come – came   ④ make – made
⑤ plan – planed

2
① do – did   ② go – went
③ lose – lost   ④ hit – hitted
⑤ drink – drank

[3-5] 빈칸에 들어갈 말로 알맞은 것을 고르시오.

3

Jenny _____ angry at me yesterday.

① is   ② was   ③ were
④ isn't   ⑤ didn't

4

I _____ for the exam last night.

① study   ② studies
③ am studying   ④ didn't study
⑤ wasn't study

5

Steve _____ to school yesterday.

① run   ② ran   ③ runs
④ runned   ⑤ didn't ran

6 빈칸에 들어갈 말이 나머지 넷과 다른 것은?

① I _____ tired yesterday.
② He _____ in London in 2018.
③ You _____ late for class yesterday.
④ There _____ a tree here a year ago.
⑤ The food _____ delicious last night.

7 빈칸에 공통으로 들어갈 말은?

· Amy, _____ you go shopping yesterday?
· They _____ not enjoy the party last night.

① do   ② did   ③ are
④ was   ⑤ were

8 빈칸에 들어갈 말로 알맞지 않은 것은?

Helen was in the office _____.

① now   ② at five
③ last Friday   ④ yesterday
⑤ an hour ago

9 다음 우리말을 영어로 바르게 옮긴 것은?

우리는 어제 외출하지 않았다.

① We not went out yesterday.
② We went not out yesterday.
③ We did not go out yesterday.
④ We weren't go out yesterday.
⑤ We did not went out yesterday.

10 다음 문장을 의문문으로 바르게 고친 것은?

> She moved to L.A. last year.

① Is she moved to L.A. last year?
② Did she move to L.A. last year?
③ Was she move to L.A. last year?
④ Did she moved to L.A. last year?
⑤ Does she moved to L.A. last year?

서술형

[11-12] 빈칸에 알맞은 말을 써서 대화를 완성하시오.

11
> A: Was the book interesting?
> B: No, _____ _____.

12
> A: Did Paul and Jane paint the wall?
> B: Yes, _____ _____.

[13-14] 다음 중 어법상 옳지 <u>않은</u> 문장을 고르시오.

13 ① I got up early this morning.
    ② We visited Australia in 2018.
    ③ They buy a house last month.
    ④ The man goes for a walk every day.
    ⑤ Mike does his homework after school.

14 ① My dad isn't a good cook.
    ② The kids are at the park now.
    ③ Kate and I weren't best friends.
    ④ She was a little girl at that time.
    ⑤ We are in Boston two years ago.

서술형

[15-17] 우리말과 일치하도록 ( ) 안의 말을 이용하여 문장을 완성하시오.

15
> 그는 오래 전에 유명한 배우였다. (a famous actor)

→ _____

a long time ago.

16
> Ryan은 그의 새 스마트폰을 땅에 떨어뜨렸다.
> (drop, his new smartphone)

→ _____

on the ground.

17
> 네가 이 상자를 바닥에 두었니? (put, this box)

→ _____

on the floor?

CHAPTER
03

Future Time
미래 표현

LET'S LOOK

I **will** be a scientist in the future.

I **am going to** meet Tom next week.

미래형은 '~할 것이다, ~할 예정이다'의 의미로 미래의 일에 대한 예측이나 주어의 의지, 계획 등을 나타낸다. 주로 「will + 동사원형」 또는 「be going to + 동사원형」 형태로 나타낸다.

UNIT 06

미래 표현 1: Will
Future Time 1: *Will*

1 will

'~할 것이다'의 의미로 미래의 일에 대한 예측이나 주어의 의지를 나타낸다.

It **will** rain tomorrow.

Don't worry. I **will** help you.

> **NOTE** 미래형은 주로 tomorrow(내일), next ~(다음 ~), 「in + 시간」(~ 후에), soon(곧) 등 미래를 나타내는 시간 표현과 함께 쓰인다.
>
> I will call you *tomorrow*.　　　　　　She will be 12 years old *next year*.
>
> The class will begin *in 10 minutes*.　　He will get better *soon*.

2 will의 긍정문과 부정문

긍정문은 주어의 인칭과 수에 관계없이 「will + 동사원형」 형태로 쓴다. 부정문은 will 뒤에 not을 붙인다.

긍정문			부정문		
주어	will (= 'll)	동사원형	주어	will not (= won't)	동사원형

We **will travel** to Australia next summer.

I am hungry. I**'ll make** a sandwich.

Jessica **will not stay** at home today.

I **won't tell** your secret to anyone. I promise.

3 will의 의문문

의문문은 주어의 인칭과 수에 관계없이 「Will + 주어 + 동사원형?」 형태로 쓴다.

의문문			긍정의 대답	부정의 대답
Will	주어	동사원형?	Yes, 주어 + will.	No, 주어 + won't.

A: **Will Amy like** the present?

B: **Yes, she will. / No, she won't.**

A: **Will you be** in class tomorrow?

B: **Yes, I will. / No, I won't.**

LET'S CHECK

A 빈칸에 will 또는 won't를 넣어 문장을 완성하세요.

0   Lucy is sleepy. She _____will_____ go to bed early.

1   It is Sunday tomorrow. We _____ go to school.

2   Kate doesn't like sweets. She _____ eat the chocolate.

3   Paul has a cold. He _____ stay at home today.

4   I am in a hurry. I _____ have breakfast.

5   It is dusty outside. I _____ close the window.

6   My grandfather is 79 years old. He _____ be 80 next year.

7   Sorry, Mr. Jones. I _____ be late again.

8   Tom broke his leg. He _____ climb the mountain.

9   James isn't good at singing. He _____ be a singer.

B 보기에서 알맞은 말을 골라 will과 함께 써서 대화를 완성하세요. (단, 한 번씩만 쓸 것)

보기	be	do	join	~~get~~	go

0   A: _____Will_____ Mike _____get_____ a new job soon?
    B: Yes, he will.

1   A: _____ you _____ us for dinner?
    B: No, I won't.

2   A: _____ robots _____ all the housework in 2050?
    B: Yes, they will.

3   A: _____ you and Mina _____ hiking tomorrow?
    B: No, we won't.

4   A: _____ it _____ sunny this weekend?
    B: Yes, it will.

WORDS   **A** dusty 먼지가 많은   climb 오르다, 등반하다   be good at ~을 잘하다   **B** join 가입하다, 함께 하다   housework 가사, 집안일

LET'S PRACTICE

A 보기에서 알맞은 말을 골라 will과 함께 써서 문장을 완성하세요. (단, 한 번씩만 쓸 것)

보기	be	miss	~~rain~~	visit

0 Take your umbrella. It _____ will rain _____ this evening.

1 Bob _____ his hometown next summer.

2 The weather _____ hot this summer.

3 Bye, Sarah. We _____ you so much.

보기	do	sell	rise	write

4 Don't worry. You _____ well on the test.

5 It's my sister's birthday. I _____ a card for her.

6 Joe needs money. He _____ his car.

7 The sun _____ at 7:00 a.m. tomorrow.

B 주어진 문장을 will을 이용하여 미래형으로 바꿔 쓰세요.

0 Jessica goes to school. → Jessica _____ will go _____ to school.

1 They are happy. → They _____ happy.

2 My uncle lives in Germany. → My uncle _____ in Germany.

3 Dad comes home early. → Dad _____ home early.

4 The bus doesn't leave on time. → The bus _____ on time.

5 He doesn't like the movie. → He _____ the movie.

6 Are you busy today? → _____ busy today?

7 Does Tina eat fish? → _____ fish?

WORDS A miss 그리워하다 hometown 고향 do well on ~을 잘하다, 잘 보다 Germany 독일

C 그림을 보고 will과 ( ) 안의 말을 이용하여 대화를 완성하세요.

0
A: _____Will_____ the concert _____begin_____ soon? (begin)
B: Yes, _____it will_____.

1
A: _____ you _____ your homework? (do)
B: Yes, _____.

2
A: _____ Nancy _____ the race? (win)
B: No, _____.

3
A: _____ Mike _____ the hospital soon? (leave)
B: No, _____.

D 밑줄 친 부분을 바르게 고치세요.

0	Robert will <u>comes</u> to the wedding.	→ come
1	The taxi will <u>is</u> here in 10 minutes.	→
2	Will you <u>closed</u> the window?	→
3	We <u>won't not</u> go there by bus.	→
4	I'll <u>having</u> chicken soup for dinner.	→
5	<u>You will</u> come to my house tomorrow?	→
6	I <u>not will</u> eat anything at night.	→

WORDS C begin 시작하다 race 경주 leave the hospital 퇴원하다 D wedding 결혼식

미래 표현 2: Be going to
Future Time 2: *Be going to*

1

be going to

'~할 것이다, ~할 예정이다'의 의미로 미래의 일에 대한 예측이나 예정된 계획을 나타낸다.

It **is going to** rain tomorrow.

I **am going to** visit my aunt this weekend.

> ✎ **NOTE** 미래의 일에 대한 예측에는 will과 be going to를 모두 쓸 수 있지만, 예정된 계획에는 be going to, 말하는 시점에 내린 결정에는 will을 쓴다.
> A: We **are going to** move next Saturday.
> B: I'm free that day. **I'll help** you.

2

be going to의 긍정문과 부정문

긍정문은 「be going to + 동사원형」의 형태이며, be동사는 주어의 인칭과 수에 따라 달라진다. 부정문은 be동사 뒤에 not을 붙인다.

긍정문				부정문			
I	am			I	am not		
You	are	going to	동사원형	You	are not	going to	동사원형
He	is			He	is not		

I **am going to get** a haircut tomorrow.

They **are going to visit** us next weekend.

We're **not going to take** the bus.

Chris **isn't going to watch** TV tonight.

3

be going to의 의문문

의문문은 「Be동사 + 주어 + going to + 동사원형?」 형태로 쓴다.

의문문				긍정의 대답	부정의 대답
Am	I			Yes, 주어 +	No, 주어 +
Are	you	going to	동사원형?	am/are/is.	'm not/aren't/isn't.
Is	he				

A: **Are you going to buy** a new table?

B: **Yes, I am. / No, I'm not.**

A: **Is she going to be** late tomorrow?

B: **Yes, she is. / No, she isn't.**

LET'S CHECK

A   ( ) 안에서 알맞은 말을 고르세요.

0   It ((is), be) going to be hot today.

1   My sister and I (am, are) going to clean the house.

2   Watch out! You (going to, are going to) fall down.

3   Angela is going to (study, studies) English grammar.

4   I'm (will, going to) practice the piano.

5   (Are, Is) Amy's friends going to visit her in the hospital?

6   The bus is going (arriving, to arrive) soon.

7   We (won't, aren't) going to meet tomorrow.

8   (Will, Are) you going to join the book club?

9   Is she going to (have, has) lunch with her friend?

B   be going to와 ( ) 안의 말을 이용하여 문장을 완성하세요.

0   She _____ is going to go _____ to the beach tomorrow. (go)

1   Joe and Stella _____ married next month. (get)

2   I _____ dinner this evening. (cook)

3   The students _____ a test tomorrow. (take)

4   Tom _____ his parents on Friday. (see)

5   We _____ by train. (not, travel)

6   The movie _____ soon. (not, start)

7   _____ the sports car? (he, buy)

8   _____ at the library? (you, study)

9   _____ for Mike? (we, wait)

WORDS   **A** Watch out! 조심해! fall down 넘어지다   **B** travel 여행하다 by train 기차로

LET'S PRACTICE

A 그림을 보고 보기에서 알맞은 말을 골라 be going to와 함께 써서 문장을 완성하세요. (단, 한 번씩만 쓸 것)

보기	buy	eat	go	mail	rain	take

0

We ___are going to go___ camping.

1

It _____.

2

She _____ a package.

3

He _____ pizza.

4

They _____ a taxi.

5

She _____ a new coat.

B be going to와 ( ) 안의 말을 이용하여 긍정문 또는 부정문을 완성하세요.

0 Tom has a toothache. He ___is going to go___ to the dentist. (go)

1 Robert is tired. He _____ today. (exercise)

2 These clothes are dirty. I _____ them. (wash)

WORDS A go camping 캠핑 가다 mail a package 소포를 부치다 B toothache 치통 go to the dentist 치과에 가다
exercise 운동하다 dirty 더러운 comfortable 편안한 repairman 수리공

3 We have a test tomorrow. We _____ tonight. (study)

4 The dog is thirsty. It _____ water. (drink)

5 Emily likes her hairstyle. She _____ it. (change)

6 These shoes aren't comfortable. I _____ them. (buy)

7 Jim plays the piano very well. He _____ a great pianist. (be)

8 Sue bought a pretty dress. She _____ it to the party. (wear)

9 The TV doesn't work. I _____ the repairman. (call)

C 그림을 보고 be going to와 ( ) 안의 말을 이용하여 대화를 완성하세요.

0
A: _____Is_____ Janet _____going to make_____ a cake? (make)
B: Yes, _____she is_____.

1
A: _____ they _____ a trip to Hawaii?
(take)
B: No, _____.

2
A: _____ Mr. and Mrs. Jones _____
the kitchen? (paint)
B: Yes, _____.

3
A: _____ he _____ a suit? (wear)
B: No, _____.

WORDS   C take a trip 여행하다

STEP 1

빈칸 완성 보기에서 알맞은 말을 골라 ( ) 안의 말과 함께 써서 문장을 완성하세요.

| 보기 | be | join | meet | tell | travel |

1 나는 언젠가 조종사가 될 것이다. (will)

→ I ＿＿＿＿ ＿＿＿＿ a pilot someday.

2 우리는 극장에서 만날 것이다. (be going to)

→ We ＿＿＿＿ ＿＿＿＿ ＿＿＿＿ ＿＿＿＿ at the theater.

3 나는 다시는 거짓말 하지 않을 것이다. (will)

→ I ＿＿＿＿ ＿＿＿＿ a lie again.

4 너는 그 동아리에 가입할거니? (be going to)

→ ＿＿＿＿ ＿＿＿＿ ＿＿＿＿ ＿＿＿＿ ＿＿＿＿ the club?

5 우리는 차로 여행하지 않을 것이다. (be going to)

→ We ＿＿＿＿ ＿＿＿＿ ＿＿＿＿ ＿＿＿＿ by car.

STEP 2

어구 배열 우리말과 일치하도록 ( ) 안의 말을 알맞게 배열하세요.

6 우리는 최선을 다할 것이다. (will, best, we, do, our)

→ ＿＿＿＿＿＿＿＿＿＿＿＿＿＿＿＿＿＿＿＿＿＿

7 그는 내 말을 듣지 않을 것이다. (he, listen to, won't, me)

→ ＿＿＿＿＿＿＿＿＿＿＿＿＿＿＿＿＿＿＿＿＿＿

8 너는 오늘밤 콘서트에 갈 거니? (go, will, to, the, you, concert)

→ ＿＿＿＿＿＿＿＿＿＿＿＿＿＿＿＿＿＿ tonight?

9 나는 이번 여름에 중국어를 배울 것이다. (I, going, Chinese, to, learn, am)

→ ＿＿＿＿＿＿＿＿＿＿＿＿＿＿＿＿＿＿ this summer.

10 그는 그의 직장을 그만두지 않을 것이다. (to, not, his, going, quit, he, job, is)

→ ＿＿＿＿＿＿＿＿＿＿＿＿＿＿＿＿＿＿＿＿＿＿

영작하기 ( ) 안의 말을 이용하여 우리말을 영어로 옮기세요.

11 사람들은 미래에 우주로 여행을 할 것이다. (will, travel into, space)

→ _____ in the future.

12 우리는 7시까지 그를 기다릴 것이다. (will, wait for, until 7 o'clock)

→ _____

13 제가 여행 가방을 대신 옮겨드릴게요. (will, carry, the suitcase, for you)

→ _____

14 나는 포기하지 않을 것이다. (will, give up)

→ _____

15 그들이 제시간에 도착할까? (will, arrive, on time)

→ _____

16 서둘러. 우린 통학 버스를 놓칠거야. (be going to, miss, the school bus)

→ Hurry up. _____

17 우리는 박물관으로 견학을 갈 것이다. (be going to, go on a field trip, to the museum)

→ _____

18 나의 형은 대학에서 법학을 공부할 것이다. (be going to, study, law, at university)

→ _____

19 Susan은 오늘 아침에 커피를 마시지 않을 것이다. (be going to, drink, coffee, this morning)

→ _____

20 그는 오늘밤 연설을 할 거니? (be going to, give a speech, tonight)

→ _____

REVIEW TEST
CHAPTER 03

[1-3] 두 문장의 뜻이 같도록 할 때 빈칸에 알맞은 말을 쓰시오.

1

I will read fifty books this year.

→ I _____ _____ _____
read fifty books this year.

2

Jeff will not sell his car.

→ Jeff _____ _____
_____ _____ sell his car.

3

Will you play soccer after school?

→ _____ _____ _____
_____ play soccer after school?

4 빈칸에 들어갈 말로 알맞은 것은?

She will _____.

① to be a doctor
② practiced the piano
③ studies for an exam
④ visiting the art museum
⑤ not go to the gym today

[5-6] 다음 우리말을 영어로 바르게 옮긴 것을 고르시오.

5

너는 이 컴퓨터를 쓸거니?

① Are you be using this computer?
② Are you going use this computer?
③ Are you going to use this computer?
④ Will you going to use this computer?
⑤ Will you be going to use this computer?

6

나는 그 질문에 대답하지 않을 것이다.

① I will no answer the question.
② I will not answer the question.
③ I will answer not the question.
④ I won't to answer the question.
⑤ I won't going to answer the question.

7 밑줄 친 부분의 쓰임이 나머지 넷과 다른 것은?

① He is going to take a taxi.
② We are going to have dinner.
③ She is going to draw a picture.
④ They are going to the water park.
⑤ I am going to visit my grandparents.

8 빈칸에 공통으로 들어갈 말은?

· Are they _____ move to Florida?
· Ann is _____ go shopping.

① will   ② not   ③ go to
④ won't   ⑤ going to

9 빈칸에 들어갈 말이 순서대로 바르게 짝지어진 것은?

> A: _____ it going to rain today?
> B: Yes, it is very dark and cloudy.
> A: Okay. I _____ take my
> umbrella.

① Does – will　　② Is – will

③ Is – won't　　④ Will – am

⑤ Will – will

10 다음 중 어법상 옳은 문장은?

① We won't not cancel the picnic.

② Cathy is not going to invite them.

③ Will you going to leave tomorrow?

④ Are Mary going to be late for school?

⑤ They're going to sleeping in a tent
   tonight.

11 다음 중 어법상 옳지 않은 문장은?

① We will go fishing tomorrow.

② Is the train going to arrive soon?

③ I'm not going to watch TV tonight.

④ Are you going to meet him yesterday?

⑤ John is going to quit his job this
   month.

서술형

[12-13] 어법상 틀린 부분을 찾아 바르게 고치시오.

12
> Ryan will runs in a marathon this
> summer.

_____ → _____

13
> Sumi and Jane is going to meet at
> seven.

_____ → _____

서술형

[14-16] 우리말과 일치하도록 ( ) 안의 말을 이용하여
문장을 완성하시오.

14
> 나는 공원에서 자전거를 탈 것이다.
> (be going to, ride)

→ I _____
   a bike in the park.

15
> 우리는 그 경기에 지지 않을 것이다. (will, lose)

→ We _____
   the game.

16
> 그들이 우리를 도와줄까? (be going to, help)

→ _____ us?

CHAPTER
04

Modal Verbs
조동사

LET'S LOOK

She **can** play the cello.

You **must** stop at the red light.

조동사는 동사 앞에 쓰여 능력, 추측, 허가, 조언, 의무 등의 의미를 더해주는 말이다. 자주 쓰이는 조동사에는 **can, may, should, must, have to** 등이 있다.

08 Can, May

Can, May

1 조동사

조동사는 동사 앞에 쓰여 능력, 추측, 허가, 조언, 의무 등의 의미를 더해주는 말이다. 조동사는 주어의 인칭과 수에 관계없이 형태가 같으며, 조동사 뒤에는 반드시 동사원형을 쓴다.

She **speaks** French well. 그녀는 프랑스어를 잘 한다.

→ She **can** *speak* French well. 그녀는 프랑스어를 잘 할 수 있다.

> **NOTE** She **cans** speak French well. [×]
> She can **speaks** French well. [×]

2 can

❶ can은 '~할 수 있다'의 의미로 능력이나 가능을 나타낸다. 부정문은 cannot[can't]을 쓰고, 의문문은 can을 주어 앞으로 보내서 만든다.

I **can** lift the box.

The baby **cannot[can't]** walk.

A: **Can** you play chess?

B: Yes, I **can**. / No, I **can't**.

❷ can은 '~해도 좋다'는 허가의 뜻을 나타내기도 한다.

You **can** use my umbrella.

You **can't** park in front of this building.

A: **Can** I borrow your pen?

B: Yes, you **can**. / No, you **can't**.

LET'S CHECK

A   ( ) 안에서 알맞은 말을 고르세요.

0   My brother can (run, runs) fast.

1   We can (go, going) there by bus.

2   Excuse me. (Are, Can) you speak Korean?

3   Elephants can't (fly, flying).

4   You (cannot use, can use not) my cellphone.

5   I can't (play, playing) the trumpet.

6   (Can he, He can) fix the car tomorrow?

7   I can't (answer, answered) this question. It is too difficult.

8   Alicia (cannot, not can) eat spicy food.

9   A: Can you play this song? B: No, I (can, can't).

B   빈칸에 can 또는 can't를 넣어 문장을 완성하세요.

0   Sam _____can't_____ help us. He is busy right now.

1   I am sorry, but I _____ go to your party.

2   James _____ ski. He learned it last winter.

3   It is really dark in here. I _____ see anything.

4   Cathy is left-handed. She _____ write with her left hand.

5   My uncle is a good cook. He _____ cook anything.

6   This room has a nice view. You _____ see the beach from here.

7   You are running so fast. I _____ catch you.

8   I'm still hungry. I _____ eat another sandwich.

9   I _____ wear that dress. It's too small for me.

WORDS   **A** trumpet (악기) 트럼펫 fix 고치다, 수리하다 spicy 매운 **B** learn 배우다 dark 어두운 left-handed 왼손잡이의 view 전망

3 may

❶ may는 '~일지도 모른다'의 의미로 약한 추측을 나타낸다. '~이 아닐지도 모른다'는 may not을 사용한다.

Ann won't talk to me. She **may** be angry at me.

I don't feel well. I **may not** go to work tomorrow.

❷ may는 '~해도 좋다'는 허가의 뜻을 나타내기도 한다. 이 경우, can보다 좀 더 정중한 표현이다.

You **may** leave early today.
　　　= can

You **may not** smoke in this building.
　　　= can't

A: **May** I use your camera?
　　　= Can

B: Yes, you **may**. / No, you **may not**.

+PLUS　1. **허락을 구할 때 쓰는 표현: 「May/Could/Can I + 동사원형?」**

May/Could I ~?가 Can I ~?보다 좀 더 정중한 표현이다.

May I see your driver's license?

Could I have some tea, please?

Can I borrow your notebook?

2. **상대방에게 요청할 때 쓰는 표현: 「Would/Could/Will/Can you + 동사원형?」**

Would/Could you ~?가 Will/Can you ~?보다 좀 더 정중한 표현이다.

Would you open the door?

Could you take a picture of us?

Will you wait for me here?

Can you pass me the salt?

cf. 요청할 때 'May you ~?'는 쓰지 않는다.

May you pass me the salt? [×]

LET'S CHECK

C 빈칸에 may 또는 may not을 넣어 문장을 완성하세요.

0 The weather is nice. We _____may_____ go out to play.

1 The traffic is terrible. I _____ arrive on time.

2 Ask him. He _____ know the answer.

3 Nick doesn't like sports. He _____ watch the football game.

4 The baby is crying. She _____ be hungry.

5 The car is very expensive. He _____ buy the car.

6 You _____ believe it, but the story is true.

7 He doesn't work hard. He _____ lose his job.

8 A: Do you know the man over there?

B: I'm not sure. He _____ be our new teacher.

D 밑줄 친 부분의 의미로 알맞은 것을 보기에서 고르세요.

보기	ⓐ 능력	ⓑ 추측	ⓒ 허가

0 Mark <u>can</u> play the drums.　　→　　ⓐ

1 We <u>may</u> go on vacation.　　→

2 <u>May</u> I have a seat?　　→

3 The news <u>may not</u> be true.　　→

4 Hippos <u>can't</u> jump.　　→

5 You <u>can</u> use my dictionary.　　→

6 I <u>may</u> be late for the movie.　　→

7 <u>Can</u> you make spaghetti?　　→

8 You <u>may not</u> swim here.　　→

WORDS　C traffic 교통　true 사실인　lose one's job 직장을 잃다　D go on vacation 휴가를 가다　have a seat 앉다　hippo 하마
dictionary 사전

LET'S PRACTICE

A 그림을 보고 can/can't와 ( ) 안의 말을 함께 써서 문장을 완성하세요.

0   My grandmother _____ *can knit* _____ a sweater. (knit)

1   Andrew _____ a tire. (change)

2   Rachel _____ a house. (design)

3   A rock _____ on water. (float)

B 보기에서 알맞은 말을 골라 문장을 완성하세요.

보기	~~be sick~~	have a test	have the wrong address
	be late	be cold	break it

0   Ann isn't in class today. She may _____ *be sick* _____ .

1   We may _____ next week. Let's study.

2   I may _____ . Don't wait for me.

3   Bring your coat. It may _____ in the evening.

4   Be careful with the glass. You may _____ .

5   I can't find his house. I may _____ .

WORDS   A knit 뜨다, 뜨개질을 하다   tire 타이어   design 설계하다   float 뜨다   B wrong 틀린   bring 가져오다   careful 조심하는

C ( ) 안의 말을 넣어 문장을 다시 쓰세요.

0 He is rich. (may)

→ _____He may be rich._____

1 Stella speaks two languages. (can)

→ _____

2 Jack is in his office. (may not)

→ _____

3 I remember his name. (can't)

→ _____

4 You borrow my car. (may)

→ _____

D ( ) 안의 말 중 필요한 것만 골라 우리말에 맞게 배열하세요.

0 그녀는 영어책을 읽을 수 있니? (English book, can, read, she, does, an)

→ _____Can she read an English book?_____

1 우리는 오늘 하이킹을 갈 수 없다. (may not, we, today, go, can't, hiking)

→ _____

2 이것은 Dave의 휴대전화일지도 모른다. (is, this, be, cellphone, Dave's, may)

→ _____

3 창문을 닫아도 될까요? (close, the, I, can, window, you)

→ _____

4 잔돈은 가져도 좋습니다. (keep, the, will, you, change, may)

→ _____

WORDS　C language 언어　remember 기억하다　borrow 빌리다　D change 잔돈, 거스름돈

09 Should, Must, Have to
UNIT

Should, Must, Have to

1 should

❶ should는 '~해야 한다, ~하는 것이 좋겠다'의 의미로 조언이나 충고를 나타낸다.

He **should** exercise more.

We are late. We **should** take a taxi.

❷ should not은 '~해서는 안 된다, ~하지 않는 것이 좋겠다'의 의미로, shouldn't로 줄여 쓸 수 있다.

We **should not** waste water.

You **shouldn't** go to bed so late.

❸ '~해야 할까?'라고 상대방에게 조언을 구할 때는 should를 주어 앞으로 보낸다.

A: **Should** I tell him the truth?

B: Yes, you **should**. / No, you **shouldn't**.

2 must

❶ must는 '~해야 한다'의 의미로 의무나 필요를 나타낸다.

We **must** show our passports at the airport.

It is snowing. You **must** wear a coat.

❷ must not은 '~해서는 안 된다'의 의미로 강한 금지를 나타낸다.

You **must not** press the button.

He **must not** drive too fast.

> **✎ NOTE** must는 '~임에 틀림없다'는 강한 추측의 의미로도 쓰인다. may(~일지도 모른다)보다 확신을 가지고 말할 때 쓴다.
>
> It **must** be Jane's notebook. Her name is on it.
>
> He **must not** be Tom. He is on vacation now.

C   ( ) 안에서 알맞은 말을 고르세요.

0   School starts at 9:00. I ((have to), shouldn't) get up at 8:00.

1   They (must, shouldn't) be late for school.

2   The kids (must not, have to) play with fire.

3   John is very smart. He (has to, doesn't have to) study a lot.

4   I have a headache. I (has to, should) stay in bed.

5   You (have to, shouldn't) drink that milk. It smells bad.

6   I (should, must not) return these pants. They are too small for me.

7   The restaurant is on the first floor. We (must, don't have to) take the elevator.

8   Helen (has to, shouldn't) wait for her mom. She doesn't have the keys.

9   A: Do I (must, have to) finish it right now? B: No, you don't have to.

D   밑줄 친 부분을 바르게 고치세요.

0   He must <u>passes</u> the exam.   →   pass

1   They must <u>to finish</u> this on time.   →

2   It's a holiday. I <u>have to</u> go to school.   →

3   Do we <u>must</u> take the subway?   →

4   You <u>have not to</u> pay for the food. It's free. →

5   You shouldn't <u>swimming</u> right after a meal.   →

6   You <u>must speak not</u> during the test.   →

7   Should I <u>watering</u> this plant every day?   →

8   Amy <u>musts</u> get up early tomorrow.   →

9   Kelly <u>have to</u> buy some food.   →

WORDS   C play with fire 불장난을 하다   headache 두통   D subway 지하철   free 무료의   water 물; *물을 주다

STEP 1

빈칸 완성 보기에서 알맞은 말을 골라 조동사와 함께 써서 문장을 완성하세요.

보기	ask	be	live	go	use

1 나의 할아버지는 스마트폰을 사용할 수 있다.

→ My grandfather _____ _____ a smartphone.

2 우리는 물 속에서 살 수 없다.

→ We _____ _____ underwater.

3 제가 질문 하나 해도 될까요?

→ _____ _____ _____ a question?

4 그것은 좋은 생각이 아닐지도 모른다.

→ It _____ _____ _____ a good idea.

5 그는 이번 여름에 미국에 갈지도 모른다.

→ He _____ _____ to America this summer.

STEP 2

어구 배열 우리말과 일치하도록 ( ) 안의 말을 알맞게 배열하세요.

6 너는 거기에 혼자 가면 안 된다. (you, alone, go, must, there, not)

→ _____

7 Sally는 그녀의 남동생을 돌봐야 한다. (has, her, Sally, to, take care of, brother)

→ _____

8 모두가 그 규칙들을 따라야 한다. (must, the, everyone, rules, follow)

→ _____

9 학생들은 그들의 점심을 가져올 필요가 없다. (don't, their, to, bring, have, students, lunch)

→ _____

10 너는 야채를 더 많이 먹는 것이 좋겠다. (eat, more, should, you, vegetables)

→ _____

STEP 3

영작하기 ( ) 안의 말을 이용하여 우리말을 영어로 옮기세요.

11 너는 악기를 연주할 수 있니? (play, a musical instrument)

→ _____

12 그는 Ann의 남자친구일지도 모른다. (be, Ann's boyfriend)

→ _____

13 그는 당신의 계획에 동의하지 않을지도 모른다. (agree with, your plan)

→ _____

14 제가 이 프린터를 써도 될까요? (I, use, this printer)

→ _____

15 커튼 좀 닫아주시겠어요? (you, close, the curtains)

→ _____

16 너는 이 셔츠를 드라이 클리닝해야만 한다. (dry-clean, this shirt)

→ _____

17 그녀는 다음 정류소에서 내려야 한다. (get off, at the next stop)

→ _____

18 너는 그를 믿어서는 안 된다. (believe, him)

→ _____

19 우리는 표를 살 필요가 없다. (buy, tickets)

→ _____

20 너는 이번 시험에 최선을 다 하는 것이 좋겠다. (do your best, for this exam)

→ _____

[1-2] 빈칸에 들어갈 말로 알맞은 것을 고르시오.

1

Fish _____ live on land.

① must
② should
③ cannot
④ may not
⑤ don't have to

2

I _____ see a doctor. I have a terrible headache.

① can
② may
③ should
④ has to
⑤ must not

3 빈칸에 들어갈 말로 알맞지 <u>않은</u> 것은?

My brother can _____.

① skate
② run fast
③ swims well
④ speak English
⑤ use a computer

4 밑줄 친 부분의 쓰임이 나머지 넷과 <u>다른</u> 것은?

① It <u>may</u> not be true.
② They <u>may</u> not like it.
③ We <u>may</u> miss the train.
④ You <u>may</u> go to the movies.
⑤ She <u>may</u> not agree with you.

5 다음 문장과 뜻이 같은 것은?

She is very good at singing.

① She can sing very well.
② She may sing very well.
③ She must sing very well.
④ She has to sing very well.
⑤ She should sing very well.

서술형

6 두 문장의 뜻이 같도록 할 때 빈칸에 알맞은 말을 쓰시오.

He must keep his promise.

→ He _____ _____ _____ his promise.

[7-8] 다음 우리말을 영어로 바르게 옮긴 것을 고르시오.

7

그 물은 깨끗하지 않을지도 모른다.

① The water cannot be clean.
② The water may not be clean.
③ The water must not be clean.
④ The water should not be clean.
⑤ The water isn't going to be clean.

8

불 좀 켜주시겠어요?

① Will I turn on the light?
② Can I turn on the light?
③ Do you turn on the light?
④ Can you turn on the light?
⑤ May you turn on the light?

[9-10] 빈칸에 들어갈 말로 알맞은 것을 고르시오.

9

A: I lost my bag on the subway.
B: You _____ go to the lost
and found center.

① may
② should
③ must not
④ shouldn't
⑤ don't have to

10

A: Where is Tony?
B: I'm not sure. He _____ be
in his room.

① will
② may
③ must
④ has to
⑤ shouldn't

11 빈칸에 들어갈 말로 알맞지 <u>않은</u> 것은?

A: Excuse me. Can I try this sweater
on?
B: _____

① Sure.
② Of course.
③ No problem.
④ No, you may not.
⑤ I'm sorry, but you can't.

12 다음 중 어법상 옳지 <u>않은</u> 문장은?

① Bears can climb trees.
② I may meet Susan next week.
③ They must to clean their room.
④ You shouldn't be late for school.
⑤ We have to be there by 1 o'clock.

서술형

[13-14] 우리말과 일치하도록 밑줄 친 부분을 바르게
고치시오.

13

너는 거짓말을 해서는 안 된다.
→ You <u>don't should</u> tell a lie.

→ _____

14

그들은 지금 당장 떠날 필요는 없다.
→ They <u>must not</u> leave right now.

→ _____

서술형

[15-17] 보기에서 알맞은 말을 골라 문장을 완성하시오.

보기 have to   may   must not

15

이번 크리스마스에는 눈이 올지도 모른다.

→ It _____ snow this
Christmas.

16

우리는 이 문제를 지금 해결해야 한다.

→ We _____ solve this
problem now.

17

밤에는 시끄럽게 해서는 안 된다.

→ You _____ make any noise
at night.

CHAPTER
05

Interrogatives
의문사

LET'S LOOK

When is your birthday?   **Where** are you from?   **How** do you feel today?

의문사는 '누가(who), 언제(when), 어디서(where), 무엇(what)을,
어떻게(how), 왜(why)' 등의 뜻을 가진 말이다. 의문사는 'Yes/No'로 대답할 수 없는
구체적인 정보를 묻는 의문문에 쓰인다.

10 의문사 1
Interrogatives 1

1 의문사

❶ 의문사는 '누가(who), 언제(when), 어디서(where), 무엇(what)을, 어떻게(how), 왜(why)' 등을 물을 때 쓰는 말이다. 의문사로 시작하는 의문문은 'Yes/No'로 대답하지 않는다.

A: **Who** is your brother?
B: The boy with the blue cap.

❷ 의문사 의문문은 의문사를 문장 맨 앞에 쓰고 그 뒤는 일반적인 의문문 어순을 따른다.

의문사 + be동사	의문사 + 일반동사
Who *are* they?	**Who** *do* you *live* with?
What *is* the title of the book?	**What** *does* she *have* for breakfast?

> 📝 **NOTE** 의문사 who, what이 주어로 쓰일 경우에는 바로 뒤에 동사가 와서 「의문사 + 동사 ~?」의 어순이 된다.
> <u>Mike</u> lives in that house. → **Who** *lives* in that house?
> <u>An apple</u> fell off the tree. → **What** *fell off* the tree?

2 사람을 나타내는 의문사: who, whom, whose

❶ who: '누구, 누가, 누구를'의 의미로, 사람에 대해 물을 때 쓴다.

He is <u>my uncle.</u>   → A: **Who** is he?
    = who   B: My uncle.

<u>Anna</u> made this cake.   → A: **Who** made this cake?
= who   B: Anna.

❷ whom: '누구를'의 의미로, who가 목적어로 쓰인 경우 who 대신 whom을 쓰기도 한다.

I saw <u>Susan</u> yesterday.   → A: **Who(m)** did you see yesterday?
    = who(m)   B: Susan.

❸ whose: '누구의'의 의미로, 소유에 대해 물을 때 쓴다.

This is <u>Emily's</u> room.   → A: **Whose** room is this?
      = whose   B: Emily's.

LET'S CHECK

A   우리말과 일치하도록 Who, Who(m), Whose 중 알맞은 것을 쓰세요.

0	<u>누가</u> 컴퓨터를 쓰고 있니?	→	___Who___ is using the computer?
1	그는 <u>누구를</u> 좋아하니?	→	_____ does he like?
2	이곳은 <u>누구의</u> 집이니?	→	_____ house is this?
3	너의 아버지는 <u>누구</u>시니?	→	_____ is your father?
4	너는 <u>누구를</u> 기다리고 있니?	→	_____ are you waiting for?
5	이것은 <u>누구의</u> 아이디어니?	→	_____ idea is this?
6	<u>누가</u> 그 경주에서 이겼니?	→	_____ won the race?
7	너는 <u>누구의</u> 선물을 샀니?	→	_____ present did you buy?
8	<u>누가</u> 너를 도와주었니?	→	_____ helped you?
9	너는 <u>누구를</u> 도와주었니?	→	_____ did you help?

B   밑줄 친 부분을 묻는 의문문이 되도록 빈칸에 알맞은 말을 쓰세요.

0	They are <u>famous musicians</u>.	→	___Who___ are they?
1	<u>Picasso</u> painted the picture.	→	_____ painted the picture?
2	She met <u>her friend</u>.	→	_____ did she meet?
3	This is <u>my</u> smartphone.	→	_____ smartphone is this?
4	<u>Henry</u> can play the guitar.	→	_____ can play the guitar?
5	That is <u>my father's</u> car.	→	_____ car is that?
6	<u>Tom</u> is sitting next to you.	→	_____ is sitting next to you?
7	Sally is talking to <u>her sister</u>.	→	_____ is Sally talking to?
8	I went camping with <u>Jake</u>.	→	_____ did you go camping with?
9	I borrowed <u>Ben's</u> umbrella.	→	_____ umbrella did you borrow?

WORDS   **A** wait for ~을 기다리다   **B** famous 유명한   musician 음악가

3 사물을 나타내는 의문사: what, which

❶ what: '무엇'의 의미로, 사물 또는 사람의 이름, 직업 등을 물을 때 쓴다. 「what + 명사」는 '무슨 ~, 어떤 ~'의 의미이다.

Her name is <u>Julie</u>.   →   A: **What** is her name?
        = what   B: Julie.

I like <u>strawberries</u>.   →   A: **What fruit** do you like?
   = what fruit   B: Strawberries.

> **✎ NOTE**   1. **직업을 묻는 표현**
> A: What is your job? / What do you do? / What do you do for a living?
> B: I'm a writer.
>
>   2. **what kind of ~: 어떤 종류의 ~**
> A: What kind of food do you like?
> B: I like Korean food.

❷ which: '어느 것'의 의미로, 정해진 대상 중에서 선택을 물을 때 쓴다. what처럼 뒤에 명사가 올 수 있으며 '어느 ~'의 뜻이다.

My jacket is <u>the blue one</u>.   →   A: **Which** is your jacket?
           = which   B: The blue one.

<u>Bus number 11</u> goes downtown.   →   A: **Which bus** goes downtown?
  = which bus   B: Bus number 11.

> **✎ NOTE**   **what vs. which**
>
> what은 선택의 범위가 없는 경우에 쓰고, which는 선택의 범위가 정해져 있거나 'Which do you like better, A or B?'처럼 질문 뒤에 선택사항을 제시하는 경우에 쓴다.
>
> A: **What** is your name?   B: My name is Sarah.
> A: **Which** is your name, *Sarah or Jessica*?   B: I'm Sarah.

LET'S CHECK

C

( ) 안에서 알맞은 말을 고르세요.

0   ((What), Which) is your phone number?

1   (What, Which) bike is yours, the red one or the blue one?

2   (What, Which) is that in the sky?

3   (What, Which) is your favorite food?

4   (What, Which) picture did you paint, the left one or the right one?

5   (What, Which) does your father do?

6   (What, Which) do you live in, a house or an apartment?

7   (What, Which) country did you visit?

8   (What, Which) country did you visit, Greece or Italy?

D

보기에서 알맞은 말을 골라 what 또는 which와 함께 써서 문장을 완성하세요.

보기	dish	color	kind	size	~~sports~~

0   A: _____What_____ _____sports_____ can you play?

   B: I can play tennis and baseball.

1   A: _____ _____ did you order, the pizza or the pasta?

   B: I ordered the pizza.

2   A: _____ _____ of movies do you like?

   B: I like action movies.

3   A: _____ _____ did you choose, red or green?

   B: I chose green.

4   A: _____ _____ do you wear?

   B: I wear a size 7.

WORDS   D dish 접시; *요리   apartment 아파트   order 주문하다   choose 고르다, 선택하다

LET'S PRACTICE

A 빈칸에 알맞은 의문사를 써서 대화를 완성하세요.

0 A: _____Who_____ is that man? B: My uncle.

1 A: _____ is Kevin doing? B: He's reading a book.

2 A: _____ do you need? B: A pen and paper.

3 A: _____ book is yours? B: The red one.

4 A: _____ birthday is it? B: My father's.

5 A: _____ way is the museum? B: To the left.

6 A: _____ letter did you receive? B: Jimmy's

7 A: _____ does Jane want? B: A cup of tea.

8 A: _____ wants a cup of tea? B: Jane.

B 그림을 보고 빈칸에 알맞은 의문사를 써서 문장을 완성하세요.

0

_____What_____ are those?

1

_____ are these people in this photo?

2

_____ bus should we take?

3

_____ notebook is this?

4

_____ hat is yours?

5

_____ is he looking for?

WORDS A receive 받다 B notebook 노트, 공책 look for 찾다

C 밑줄 친 부분을 묻는 의문문이 되도록 빈칸에 알맞은 말을 쓰세요.

0 A: _What_ _are_ _they_ doing?

B: They are playing volleyball.

1 A: _____ _____ answer my question?

B: I can answer your question.

2 A: _____ _____ _____ see last night?

B: We saw a car accident last night.

3 A: _____ _____ are these?

B: These are my sister's gloves.

4 A: _____ _____ _____ like better, cats or dogs?

B: I like cats better.

D 우리말과 일치하도록 ( ) 안의 말을 알맞게 배열하세요.

0 누가 내 케이크를 먹었니? (cake, ate, my)

→ Who _ate my cake_ ?

1 당신은 누구와 함께 사나요? (with, you, live, do)

→ Who(m) _____ ?

2 그들은 누구의 친구들이니? (they, friends, are)

→ Whose _____ ?

3 너는 무슨 과목을 좋아하니? (you, subject, like, do)

→ What _____ ?

4 어느 자리가 그녀의 것이니? (hers, is, seat)

→ Which _____ ?

11 의문사 2
Interrogatives 2

1 시간, 때를 묻는 의문사: when

'언제'의 의미로, 때를 물을 때 쓴다.

Their wedding is next Saturday. → A: **When** is their wedding?
= when B: It's next Saturday.

I met Jane yesterday. → A: **When** did you meet Jane?
= when B: Yesterday.

NOTE 구체적인 시간, 날짜, 요일을 물을 때는 when 대신 「what + time/date/day」를 쓰기도 한다
A: **What time** does the game start? 〈시간〉 B: At 6 o'clock.
A: **What date** is it? 〈날짜〉 B: It's May 17.
A: **What day** is it? 〈요일〉 B: It's Thursday.

2 장소를 묻는 의문사: where

'어디'의 의미로, 위치, 장소 등을 물을 때 쓴다.

Dad is in the kitchen. → A: **Where** is Dad?
= where B: In the kitchen.

They are going to the park. → A: **Where** are they going?
= where B: They're going to the park.

3 이유를 묻는 의문사: why

'왜'의 의미로, 이유를 물을 때 쓴다. 대답에는 주로 because(왜냐하면)가 사용된다.

My brother is angry at me → A: **Why** is your brother angry at you?
because I lost his watch. B: *Because* I lost his watch.
= why

I stayed at home → A: **Why** did you stay at home?
because I didn't feel well. B: *Because* I didn't feel well.
= why

LET'S CHECK

A ( ) 안에서 알맞은 말을 고르세요.

0 A: (When, (Where)) does she live?   B: On Main Street.

1 A: (When, Where) were you born?   B: In 2005.

2 A: (When, Where) can I visit you?   B: Anytime is fine.

3 A: (When, Where) can I buy stamps?   B: At the post office.

4 A: (Why, When) is Betty in the hospital?   B: She broke her arm.

5 A: (Why, When) is he tired?   B: Because he worked late.

6 A: (Why, When) does your flight leave?   B: At 7:00 p.m.

7 A: (Why, When) does he go to the gym?   B: After work.

8 A: (Why, Where) are you crying?   B: Because the movie is sad.

9 A: (Why, Where) is the Amazon River?   B: It's in South America.

B 밑줄 친 부분을 묻는 의문문이 되도록 빈칸에 알맞은 말을 쓰세요.

0 The finial exam is on Friday.

→ _____When_____ is the final exam?

1 Your boots are under the table.

→ _____ are my boots?

2 I am reading the book because it's interesting.

→ _____ are you reading the book?

3 The children watched TV in the living room.

→ _____ did the children watch TV?

4 She is going to leave next Monday.

→ _____ is she going to leave?

WORDS   **A** anytime 언제든지   stamp 우표   **B** boot 장화, 부츠

4 상태, 수단, 방법을 묻는 의문사: how

'어떤, 어떻게'의 의미로, 상태, 수단, 방법 등을 물을 때 쓴다.

I'm <u>fine</u> today.　　　　　　　　　　　→　　A: **How** are you today?
　　= how　　　　　　　　　　　　　　　　　　　 B: I'm fine.

James goes to school <u>by bus</u>.　　　　　→　　A: **How** does James go to school?
　　　　　　　　　　= how　　　　　　　　　　　 B: By bus.

> **✎ NOTE**　상대방에게 '어떻게 생각해?'라고 의견을 물을 때는 how 대신 what을 쓴다.
> **How** do you think about the idea? [×]
> **What** do you think about the idea? [○]

5 how + 형용사/부사

❶ 의문사 how는 「how + 형용사/부사」의 형태로 쓰여 '얼마나 ～한/하게'의 의미를 나타낸다.

how old	몇 살의	**How old** are you?
how often	얼마나 자주	**How often** do you go to the movies?
how far	얼마나 먼	**How far** is the subway station from here?
how tall	얼마나 키가 큰 얼마나 높은	**How tall** is your sister? **How tall** is this building?
how long	얼마나 긴 얼마나 오래	**How long** is the Brooklyn Bridge in New York? **How long** will you stay here?
how much	얼마(의)	**How much** is this jacket?

❷ 수나 양이 얼마인지는 「how many + 복수명사」 또는 「how much + 셀 수 없는 명사」의 형태로 묻는다.

How many oranges are there?

How much time do we have?

> **✎ NOTE**　how many times: 몇 번
> **How many times** do you go shopping each week?
> **How many times** did you water the plant today?

LET'S CHECK

C 주어진 의문사와 대답을 알맞게 연결하세요.

0 How long? •————————————• ⓐ Three meters long.

1 How much? •   • ⓑ 26 years old.

2 How often? •   • ⓒ Four.

3 How old? •   • ⓓ Once a week.

4 How tall? •   • ⓔ By subway.

5 How many? •   • ⓕ Fifteen dollars.

6 How far? •   • ⓖ 178cm tall.

7 How? •   • ⓗ A five-minute walk from here.

D 빈칸에 How many 또는 How much를 넣어 문장을 완성하세요.

0 _____How much_____ paint do we need?

1 _____ bread do you want?

2 _____ rooms are there in this house?

3 _____ glasses are there on the table?

4 _____ water is there in the bottle?

5 _____ children do they have?

6 _____ sugar do you want in your tea?

7 _____ books do you read in a year?

8 _____ time do you need?

9 _____ times do you eat out in a month?

WORDS   C a five-minute walk 걸어서 5분   D bottle 병   eat out 외식하다

LET'S PRACTICE

A ( ) 안에서 알맞은 말을 고르세요.

0   (When, (Where)) is the grocery store?

1   (When, How) is the next national holiday?

2   (How, Why) do you feel today?

3   (Why, Where) are you going there?

4   (Where, How far) is the beach from here?

5   How (far, long) did he take a nap?

6   How (far, often) do you get a haircut?

7   How (tall, long) is the Eiffel Tower?

8   How (much, many) rice is in this jar?

9   How (much, many) hours did they watch TV?

B 그림을 보고 보기에서 알맞은 말을 골라 의문문을 완성하세요.

0    1    2    3

보기	How far	How many	How much	How tall

0   ___How tall___ are you?

1   _____ sheep can you see?

2   _____ is the moon from the Earth?

3   _____ is this scarf?

C 자연스러운 대화가 되도록 질문에 맞는 대답을 고르세요.

0   How was your trip? ___ⓘ___   ⓐ On Pine Street.

1   How is the weather? _____   ⓑ It's for a week.

2   Why did you buy that? _____   ⓒ It's sunny.

3   Where are they from? _____   ⓓ By train.

4   How will you go to Busan? _____   ⓔ Five years ago.

5   Where is your school? _____   ⓕ Because it was cheap.

6   How do you spell your name? _____   ⓖ They're from France.

7   When did you first fly on a plane? _____   ⓗ S-A-R-A-H.

8   How old is this church? _____   ⓘ It was fantastic!

9   How long is your spring vacation? _____   ⓙ About 100 years old.

D 우리말과 일치하도록 빈칸에 알맞은 말을 써서 문장을 완성하세요.

0   너는 얼마나 자주 이를 닦니?

→ ___How___ ___often___ do you brush your teeth?

1   너는 몇 시에 학교에 가니?

→ _____ _____ do you go to school?

2   그는 왜 서두르니?

→ _____ is he in a hurry?

3   어제는 무슨 요일이었니?

→ _____ _____ was it yesterday?

4   너는 그에 대해 어떻게 생각하니?

→ _____ do you think about him?

WORDS   A trip 여행   spell 철자를 말하다[쓰다]   church 교회

STEP 1

빈칸 완성 보기에서 알맞은 말을 골라 문장을 완성하세요.

보기	who	whose	how	what	which

1 누가 저녁을 요리할거니?

→ _____ will cook dinner?

2 그는 여가 시간에 무엇을 하니?

→ _____ does he do in his free time?

3 이것은 누구의 교복이니?

→ _____ uniform is this?

4 녹차와 커피 중 어느 것을 원하세요?

→ _____ do you want, green tea or coffee?

5 그 식당의 음식은 어땠니?

→ _____ was the food at the restaurant?

STEP 2

어구 배열 우리말과 일치하도록 ( ) 안의 말을 알맞게 배열하세요.

6 다음에 무슨 일이 생길 것인가? (happen, next, what, will)

→ _____

7 이 단어는 무슨 뜻이니? (what, mean, word, this, does)

→ _____

8 너는 얼마나 멀리 뛸 수 있니? (jump, far, can, how, you)

→ _____

9 너는 얼마나 자주 수영 하러 가니? (swimming, often, you, how, do, go)

→ _____

10 너는 어디에 네 사진들을 보관하니? (you, keep, pictures, where, do, your)

→ _____

STEP 3 · 영작하기 ( ) 안의 말을 이용하여 우리말을 영어로 옮기세요.

11 오늘은 무슨 요일이니? (day, it, today)

→ _____

12 그 팀의 주장은 누구니? (the captain of the team)

→ _____

13 너는 크리스마스에 무엇을 원하니? (want, for Christmas)

→ _____

14 그들은 어디를 가고 있니? (go)

→ _____

15 네 여동생은 몇 살이니? (your sister)

→ _____

16 한강은 길이가 얼마인가요? (the Han River)

→ _____

17 너는 언제 숙제를 끝냈니? (finish, your homework)

→ _____

18 그들은 왜 일찍 떠났니? (leave, early)

→ _____

19 너는 한 달에 돈을 얼마나 쓰니? (money, spend, in a month)

→ _____

20 너는 어젯밤에 몇 시간을 잤니? (hour, sleep, last night)

→ _____

REVIEW TEST
CHAPTER 05

[1-3] 빈칸에 들어갈 말로 알맞은 것을 고르시오.

1

A: _____ did you have for dinner?
B: I had spaghetti.

① How   ② Who   ③ What
④ When   ⑤ Where

2

A: _____ cat is yours?
B: The black one.

① Who   ② What   ③ Whom
④ Whose   ⑤ Which

3

A: _____ did you go to the gym?
B: I walked.

① Who   ② Why   ③ How
④ When   ⑤ Where

서술형

4 두 문장의 뜻이 같도록 할 때 빈칸에 알맞은 말을 쓰시오.

What time does the movie start?

→ _____ does the movie start?

서술형

[5-7] 보기에서 알맞은 말을 골라 대화를 완성하시오.

보기   who   why   where

5

A: _____ is your sister?
B: She's in her bedroom.

6

A: _____ broke the flowerpot?
B: John did.

7

A: _____ are you happy?
B: Our team won the game.

8 빈칸에 들어갈 말이 나머지 넷과 <u>다른</u> 것은?

① _____ is the weather?
② _____ do you feel today?
③ _____ does "VIP" mean?
④ _____ does she go to work?
⑤ _____ do you spell your name?

9 빈칸에 공통으로 들어갈 말은?

· _____ is the computer?
· _____ orange juice do we have?

① How old   ② How fast
③ How often   ④ How many
⑤ How much

10 다음 중 대화가 자연스러운 것은?

① A: Why are you late?
B: Yes, I am.
② A: How do you go to the mall?
B: On Sundays.
③ A: What does your mother do?
B: She's a fashion designer.
④ A: How often does she drink coffee?
B: In the coffee shop.
⑤ A: How long is the Great Wall in China?
B: It was fantastic.

[11-12] 밑줄 친 부분이 잘못된 것을 고르시오.

11 ① How is your mother?
② Where are they from?
③ What is Hannah doing?
④ Why did they come here?
⑤ Who is your father's name?

12 ① How many chairs are there?
② How many people are there?
③ How much soda did he drink?
④ How many towels do you want?
⑤ How much times did he call you?

서술형

[13-14] ( ) 안의 말을 알맞게 배열하여 문장을 완성하시오.

13 (tall, how, this, is, building)

→ _____

14 (like, do, what, you, of, music, kind)

→ _____

서술형

[15-17] 우리말과 일치하도록 ( ) 안의 말을 이용하여 문장을 완성하시오.

15 Johns 선생님은 무슨 과목을 가르치시니? (subject)

→ _____ does Mr. Johns teach?

16 이것은 누구의 열쇠니? (key)

→ _____ is this?

17 공항은 여기서 얼마나 머니? (far)

→ _____ is the airport from here?

CHAPTER
06
Comparisons
비교

LET'S LOOK

I am **taller** than my sister.
Dad is the **tallest** person in my family.

비교급과 **최상급**은 두 개 이상의 대상을 형용사와 부사를 이용하여 비교할 때 쓰는 표현이다. 비교급은 '**더 ~한/하게**'의 의미로 형용사/부사 끝에 주로 **-er**를 붙여 만든다. 최상급은 '**가장 ~한/하게**'의 의미로 형용사/부사 끝에 주로 **-est**를 붙여 만든다.

UNIT 12 비교급
Comparatives

1 비교급

비교급은 두 개 이상의 대상을 형용사와 부사를 이용하여 비교할 때 쓰는 표현이다. 주로 「비교급 + than」의 형태로 쓰여 '…보다 더 ～한/하게'의 의미를 나타낸다.

Rick is **tall**.

Rick is **taller than** his father.

> **✎ NOTE** 1. than 뒤에는 주로 목적격 또는 「주어 + 동사」 형태를 쓴다
>
> I am **older than** *him*.   I am **older than** *he is*.
>
> I run **faster than** *him*.   I run **faster than** *he does*.
>
> 2. 비교의 대상이 소유물인 경우, than 뒤에 소유대명사가 올 수 있다.
>
> *Her bag* is **bigger than** *me*. [×]   *Her bag* is **bigger than** *mine*. [○]
>
> *Her bag* is **bigger than** *my bag*. [○]

> **(+ PLUS)** much/still/far/even/a lot + 비교급: 훨씬 더 ～한 (very는 비교급 앞에 쓸 수 없다.)
>
> Jane is **very** *tall*. 〈원급〉
>
> Jane is **much** *taller* than her mother. 〈비교급〉

2 비교급 만드는 법

비교급은 주로 형용사/부사 끝에 -er를 붙이거나, 앞에 more를 붙여 만든다.

대부분의 경우	+ -er	old → old**er**	fast → fast**er**
-e로 끝나는 경우	+ -r	large → larg**er**	nice → nic**er**
-y로 끝나는 경우	y를 i로 고치고 + -er	easy → eas**ier**	heavy → heav**ier**
〈단모음 + 단자음〉으로 끝나는 경우	자음을 한번 더 쓰고 + -er	big → big**ger** fat → fat**ter**	hot → hot**ter** thin → thin**ner**
2, 3음절 이상인 경우, -ly로 끝나는 부사	more + 형용사/부사	**more** beautiful **more** slowly	**more** important **more** carefully
예외	good/well → **better** many/much → **more**	bad → **worse** little → **less**	

This book is **easier than** that one.

My dog is **bigger than** Mike's.

For me, good health is **more important than** money.

Susie dances **better than** Brian.

LET'S CHECK

A 주어진 단어의 비교급을 쓰세요.

0	old	_____older_____	10	cheap	_____
1	small	_____	11	expensive	_____
2	big	_____	12	warm	_____
3	famous	_____	13	cold	_____
4	easy	_____	14	high	_____
5	difficult	_____	15	lucky	_____
6	long	_____	16	good	_____
7	busy	_____	17	bad	_____
8	sweet	_____	18	many	_____
9	hot	_____	19	little	_____

B ( ) 안의 말을 이용하여 비교급 문장을 완성하세요.

0 A balloon is _____lighter_____ than a rock. (light)

1 China is _____ than India. (large)

2 This dress is _____ than that one. (pretty)

3 A cucumber is _____ than a radish. (thin)

4 The sofa is _____ than the chair. (comfortable)

5 Your English is _____ than mine. (good)

6 Susan sings _____ than Kevin. (beautifully)

7 My aunt drives _____ than my uncle. (safely)

8 He arrived at school _____ than I did. (early)

9 My father cooks _____ than my mother. (bad)

WORDS   A lucky 운이 좋은   B light 가벼운   cucumber 오이   radish 무   thin 얇은, 가는

LET'S PRACTICE

A 그림을 보고 보기에서 알맞은 말을 골라 적절한 형태로 바꾸어 비교급 문장을 완성하세요.

0  1  2  3

보기	long	small	~~tall~~	thick

0   The tree is _____ taller than _____ the house.

1   A mouse is _____ a rabbit.

2   Mary's hair is _____ Jean's.

3   The dictionary is _____ the magazine.

B ( ) 안의 말을 이용하여 비교급 문장을 만드세요.

0   (mountains / high / hills)

→ _____ Mountains are higher than hills. _____

1   (oranges / sweet / lemons)

→ _____

2   (gold / expensive / silver)

→ _____

3   (Egypt / hot / Korea)

→ _____

4   (snails / move / slowly / turtles)

→ _____

WORDS   A thick 두꺼운   B hill 언덕   silver 은   snail 달팽이   turtle 거북

C ( ) 안에서 알맞은 말을 고르세요.

0 Diamond is (hard, (harder)) than steel.

1 My father gets up (early, earlier) than me.

2 The Amazon is (wider, more wide) than the Nile.

3 I have (more, much) books than you.

4 I feel much (more good, better) than before.

5 Ron is (younger, more young) than my sister.

6 He looks (happier, more happy) than me.

7 This song is (popularer, more popular) than that one.

8 Her shoes are smaller than (me, mine).

9 Mike plays sports better than I (am, do).

D 우리말과 일치하도록 ( ) 안의 말을 이용하여 문장을 완성하세요.

0 오늘은 어제보다 날씨가 더 좋다. (good)
   → The weather today is _____better_____ than it was yesterday.

1 그는 버는 것보다 더 많은 돈을 쓴다. (much)
   → He spends _____ money than he earns.

2 그 영화는 책보다 더 좋지 않았다. (bad)
   → The movie was _____ than the book.

3 그녀는 다른 사람들보다 더 적게 먹는다. (little)
   → She eats _____ than others.

4 나의 언니는 나보다 옷이 더 많다. (many)
   → My sister has _____ clothes than I do.

WORDS C hard 힘든; *단단한 steel 강철 D earn (돈을) 벌다

13 최상급
Superlatives

1 최상급

최상급은 세 개 이상의 대상을 형용사와 부사를 이용하여 비교할 때 쓰는 표현이다. 「the + 최상급」의 형태로 쓰여 '가장 ~한/하게'의 의미를 나타낸다.

Rick is **tall**.

Rick is **taller** than his father.

Rick is **the tallest** person in his family.

> **✎ NOTE**　1. 최상급 뒤에는 기간, 장소 등의 범위가 제시되는 경우가 많다. 이 때 전치사 in, of를 주로 사용한다.
>
> 　Mt. Everest is **the highest** mountain *in the world*.
>
> 　James is **the fastest** runner *of the three*.
>
> 　2. 최상급 뒤에 오는 명사는 생략되기도 한다.
>
> 　My sister is **the youngest** (person) in my family.

2 최상급 만드는 법

최상급은 주로 형용사/부사 끝에 -est를 붙이거나, 앞에 most를 붙여 만든다.

대부분의 경우	+ -est	old → old**est**	fast → fast**est**
-e로 끝나는 경우	+ -st	large → large**st**	nice → nice**st**
-y로 끝나는 경우	y를 i로 고치고 + -est	easy → eas**iest**	heavy → heav**iest**
〈단모음 + 단자음〉으로 끝나는 경우	자음을 한번 더 쓰고 + -est	big → big**gest** fat → fat**test**	hot → hot**test** thin → thin**nest**
2, 3음절 이상인 경우, -ly로 끝나는 부사	most + 형용사/부사	**most** beautiful **most** slowly	**most** important **most** carefully
예외	good/well → **best** many/much → **most**	bad → **worst** little → **least**	

The church is **the oldest** building in this town.

The African elephant is **the heaviest** animal on land.

Summer is **the hottest** season of the year.

Mary is **the most beautiful** girl in our school.

LET'S CHECK

A 주어진 단어의 최상급을 쓰세요.

0	long	_longest_	10	cold	
1	hard		11	high	
2	big		12	funny	
3	famous		13	cheap	
4	easy		14	delicious	
5	small		15	deep	
6	beautiful		16	busy	
7	pretty		17	good	
8	smart		18	many	
9	hot		19	little	

B 보기에서 알맞은 말을 골라 적절한 형태로 바꾸어 우리말을 영어로 옮기세요.

보기	bad	difficult	late	happy	~~rich~~	short	strong	thin

0	가장 부유한 사람	→	the	_richest_	person
1	가장 짧은 영화	→	the		movie
2	가장 힘이 센 남자	→	the		man
3	가장 최신 모델	→	the		model
4	가장 얇은 책	→	the		book
5	가장 행복한 날	→	the		day
6	가장 어려운 문제	→	the		problem
7	가장 최악의 경우	→	the		case

WORDS   A deep 깊은   B late 늦은; *최근의   problem 문제

LET'S PRACTICE

A   ( ) 안의 말을 이용하여 최상급 문장을 완성하세요.

0   Greenland is _____the largest_____ island in the world. (large)

1   I ordered _____ item on the menu. (cheap)

2   This is _____ room in the hotel. (nice)

3   He is _____ soccer player in the world. (good)

4   Today is _____ day of my life. (happy)

5   Who is _____ person in your family? (tall)

6   New York is _____ city in the world. (exciting)

7   It was _____ movie of the year. (bad)

8   You are _____ boy in the world. (funny)

9   _____ bridge in the world is in China. (long)

B   그림을 보고 보기에서 알맞은 말을 골라 적절한 형태로 바꾸어 최상급 문장을 완성하세요.

0    1    2    3

| 보기 | big | expensive | ~~high~~ | short |

0   I got _____the highest_____ score in math.

1   The basketball is _____ of the three.

2   February is _____ month of the year.

3   The rose is _____ of the three.

WORDS   A island 섬   bridge 다리   B score 점수   February 2월

C　( ) 안에서 알맞은 말을 고르세요.

0　The rose is the (prettier, (prettiest)) in the garden.

1　This is the (older, oldest) temple in Korea.

2　David is (cleverer, cleverest) than his brothers.

3　David is the (cleverer, cleverest) of his brothers.

4　She is the (more, most) famous person in the town.

5　The island is the (better, best) place for a vacation.

6　April is (less, least) cold than March.

7　This song is (easier, easiest) than that one.

8　Christmas is the (busier, busiest) season of the year.

9　The new bed is (more, most) comfortable than the old one.

D　밑줄 친 부분을 바르게 고치세요.

0　France is <u>large</u> than Spain.　　　→　　larger

1　Jessica paints <u>well</u> than Mike.　　　→

2　The pizza is more delicious <u>to</u> the pasta.　　　→

3　The whale is <u>more big</u> than the elephant.　　　→

4　Kate is <u>best</u> student in the school.　　　→

5　It was the <u>wonderfulest</u> event in my life.　　　→

6　Who is the <u>nicer</u> boy of the three?　　　→

7　It was the <u>more</u> fantastic musical.　　　→

8　She is the <u>most fast</u> runner in the class.　　　→

9　Grandpa is <u>oldest</u> in my family.　　　→

WORDS　C temple 절, 사원　clever 영리한　D whale 고래

STEP 1

빈칸 완성 ( ) 안의 말을 이용하여 문장을 완성하세요.

1 이번 겨울은 작년 겨울보다 더 춥다. (cold)

→ This winter is _____ _____ last winter.

2 내 휴대용 컴퓨터는 네 것보다 더 얇다. (thin)

→ My laptop is _____ _____ yours.

3 너희 나라에서 가장 긴 강은 무엇이니? (long)

→ What is _____ _____ river in your country?

4 축구는 그 나라에서 가장 인기 있는 스포츠이다. (popular)

→ Soccer is _____ _____ _____ sport in the country.

5 나는 Jake보다 더 열심히 영어를 공부한다. (hard)

→ I study English _____ _____ Jake.

STEP 2

어구 배열 우리말과 일치하도록 ( ) 안의 말을 알맞게 배열하세요.

6 비행기는 기차보다 더 빠르다. (airplane, a, faster, is, an, than, train)

→ _____

7 그녀는 나보다 여가 시간이 더 많다. (more, she, me, has, than, free time)

→ _____

8 사자는 고양이보다 훨씬 더 위험하다. (dangerous, a, much, than, cat, is, more)

→ A lion _____

9 역사는 나에게 가장 흥미로운 과목이다. (history, the, is, interesting, subject, most)

→ _____ to me.

10 그것은 올해 최고의 아이디어이다. (best, it, idea, of, year, the, is, the)

→ _____

STEP 3

영작하기 ( ) 안의 말을 이용하여 우리말을 영어로 옮기세요.

11 태양은 달보다 더 밝다. (the sun, bright, the moon)

→ _____

12 우리 아빠는 우리 엄마보다 더 바쁘다. (my father, busy, my mother)

→ _____

13 Bill은 Mike보다 더 부지런하다. (Bill, diligent, Mike)

→ _____

14 이 웹사이트가 저 책보다 더 도움이 된다. (this website, helpful, that book)

→ _____

15 그것은 그 사무실에서 가장 오래된 컴퓨터이다. (old, computer, in the office)

→ _____

16 Julie는 그 반에서 가장 예쁜 소녀이다. (pretty, girl, in the class)

→ _____

17 과학 시험은 모든 시험들 중 가장 어려웠다. (the science test, difficult, of all the tests)

→ _____

18 그는 역사상 가장 위대한 발명가였다. (great, inventor, in history)

→ _____

19 그는 한국에서 최고의 수영 선수이다. (good, swimmer, in Korea)

→ _____

20 나는 수학에서 가장 나쁜 점수를 받았다. (get, bad, score, in math)

→ _____

1 비교급과 최상급이 잘못 연결된 것은?

① nice – nicer – nicest
② hot – hotter – hottest
③ lucky – luckier – luckiest
④ cheap – cheaper – cheapest
⑤ famous – famouser – famousest

[2-3] 빈칸에 들어갈 말로 알맞은 것을 고르시오.

2

Silk is _____ than cotton.

① soft ② softer
③ softest ④ more soft
⑤ most soft

3

He is the _____ player on the team.

① fast ② faster
③ fastest ④ more fast
⑤ most fast

서술형

[4-5] 두 문장을 비교급을 이용해서 한 문장으로 만들 때 빈칸에 알맞은 말을 쓰시오.

4

My father got up at 7:00 a.m.
I got up at 8:00 a.m.

→ My father got up _____ than me.

5

The scarf is 10,000 won.
The gloves are 15,000 won.

→ The gloves are _____ _____ than the scarf.

6 다음 우리말을 영어로 바르게 옮긴 것은?

그의 책은 내 것보다 더 두껍다.

① His book is thicker than I.
② His book is thick than mine.
③ His book is more thick than I.
④ His book is thicker than mine.
⑤ His book is thickest than mine.

7 빈칸에 들어갈 말이 순서대로 바르게 짝지어진 것은?

· This doll is _____ than that one.
· He is the _____ boy in the class.

① pretty – smart
② prettiest – smarter
③ prettier – smartest
④ prettier – most smart
⑤ more pretty – smartest

8 빈칸에 들어갈 말로 알맞지 않은 것은?

Rick looks _____ happier than Jim.

① still ② very ③ a lot
④ even ⑤ much

9 다음 표의 내용과 일치하지 <u>않는</u> 것은?

	Mike	Tom	Judy
Age	13	14	15
Weight	50kg	55kg	47kg
Height	155cm	157cm	162cm

① Tom is older than Mike.
② Judy is taller than Tom.
③ Judy is heavier than Tom.
④ Mike is shorter than Tom.
⑤ Mike is the youngest of all.

서술형

[10-11] 다음 표를 보고 ( ) 안의 말을 이용하여 문장을 완성하시오.

Toy Story 4	Aladdin	The Lion King
1h 40m	2h 10m	1h 58m

10
Toy Story 4 is _____ _____
The Lion King. (short)

11
Aladdin is _____ _____
movie of the three. (long)

12 다음 중 어법상 옳지 <u>않은</u> 문장은?

① Julie studies harder than Sam.
② Seoul is the largest city in Korea.
③ The kitten is cuter than the puppy.
④ Her room is more clean than mine.
⑤ Health is the most important of all.

서술형

[13-14] 어법상 <u>틀린</u> 부분을 찾아 바르게 고치시오.

13
She can swim more well than me.

_____ → _____

14
Luke is the stronger boy of the three.

_____ → _____

서술형

[15-17] 우리말과 일치하도록 ( ) 안의 말을 이용하여 문장을 완성하시오.

15
나의 형은 나보다 더 부지런하다. (diligent)

→ My brother is _____
me.

16
네 계획은 내 것보다 더 나쁘다. (bad)

→ Your plan is _____
mine.

17
1월은 일년 중 가장 추운 달이다. (cold, month)

→ January is _____ of
the year.

CHAPTER
07

Types of
Sentences
문장의 종류

LET'S LOOK

Close the window.

Let's eat!

How small!

It's your birthday, isn't it?

일반적인 평서문, 부정문, 의문문 외에도 명령이나 제안을 할 때, 감탄을 표현할 때,
내용을 확인하는 질문을 할 때 등 상황에 따라 다양한 종류의 문장을 쓸 수 있다.
각 문장마다 형태가 다르므로 이러한 다양한 문장 구조를 잘 익혀두도록 한다.

14 명령문, 제안문
Imperatives, Suggestions

1 명령문

상대방에게 어떤 행동을 하도록 요구하거나 지시하는 문장이다.

❶ 긍정 명령문: '～해라'의 의미로, 주어(you) 없이 동사원형으로 시작한다.

Do your homework first.

Be careful.

❷ 부정 명령문: '～하지 마라'의 의미로, 「Do not[Don't] + 동사원형」 형태로 쓴다.

Do not talk in class.

Don't be lazy.

❸ 완곡하게 표현할 때는 명령문 앞이나 뒤에 please를 붙인다.

Please sit down.

Open your book, **please**.

> ✎NOTE 명령문 + and ～: …해라, 그러면 ～할 것이다 / 명령문 + or ～: …해라, 그렇지 않으면 ～할 것이다
>   **Take** the subway, **and** you will get there in time.
>   **Take** the subway, **or** you won't get there in time.

2 제안문

상대방에게 어떤 것을 함께 하자고 제안하는 문장이다. 주로 「Let's + 동사원형」으로 나타낸다.

❶ Let's + 동사원형: '～하자'

Let's clean the house.

❷ Let's not + 동사원형: '～하지 말자'

Let's not watch the movie.

> ✎NOTE 「Why don't we + 동사원형?」/「How about + 동사원형-ing?」
>   「Let's + 동사원형」과 비슷한 표현으로 '～하는 것이 어때?'의 의미이다
>   **Why don't we play** soccer? = **How about playing** soccer?

LET'S CHECK

A 그림을 보고 보기에서 알맞은 말을 골라 명령문을 완성하세요.

보기	be	close	feed	jump	put	wake

0 ___Close___ the window.

1 _____ your hands up!

2 Don't _____ the animals.

3 _____ quiet in the library.

4 Don't _____ on the bed.

5 Juile, _____ up.

B 빈칸에 Let's 또는 Let's not을 넣어 문장을 완성하세요.

0 Dinner is ready. _____Let's_____ eat.

1 We are late. _____ take a taxi.

2 It's a nice day. _____ stay at home.

3 I'm thirsty. _____ buy some water.

4 _____ worry. Everything will be okay.

5 It's Sunday tomorrow. _____ get up early.

6 We'll go there by train. _____ meet at the station.

7 I'm going to the library. _____ go together.

WORDS   B ready 준비가 된

LET'S PRACTICE

A ( ) 안의 말을 이용하여 명령문을 완성하세요. (단, 필요하면 don't를 쓸 것)

0   _____Don't touch_____ the wall. The paint isn't dry. (touch)

1   It's too dark in here. _____ on the light. (turn)

2   Please _____ for me. I'm almost ready. (wait)

3   Jimmy, _____ nice to your brother. (be)

4   _____ this book. It's boring. (read)

5   The house is on fire! _____ 119! (call)

6   Sally, _____ some rest. You look tired. (get)

7   _____ here. This is a no-parking zone. (park)

8   Please _____ me. I don't understand this question. (help)

9   The baby is sleeping. _____ any noise. (make)

B 빈칸에 and 또는 or을 넣어 문장을 완성하세요.

0   Exercise regularly, _____and_____ you will be healthy.

1   Put on your raincoat, _____ you will get wet.

2   Go straight, _____ you will see the station.

3   Hurry up, _____ you'll miss the bus.

4   Study hard, _____ you will pass the test.

5   Set the alarm clock, _____ you will get up late.

6   Don't eat too much ice cream, _____ you will get sick.

7   Come home early, _____ we can have dinner together.

WORDS A turn on 켜다 almost 거의 be on fire 불타고 있다 park 주차하다 no-parking zone 주차 금지 구역 noise 소리, 소음
B regularly 규칙적으로 get wet (물에) 젖다 get sick 아프다, 병이 나다

C 보기에서 알맞은 말을 골라 문장을 완성하세요. (단, 한 번씩만 쓸 것)

보기	have a party	~~take a break~~	wash them
	drive slowly	cook something	cross the road

0 I feel sleepy. Why don't we _____take a break_____?

1 The traffic light is red. Don't _____.

2 I'm already hungry. Let's _____ for dinner.

3 Your hands are dirty. Go and _____.

4 It's Jane's birthday. Let's _____ for her.

5 The roads are icy. Please _____.

D 밑줄 친 부분을 바르게 고치세요.

0 Please <u>closes</u> the door. → *close*

1 <u>Careful</u>! The pot is very hot. →

2 <u>Let's we</u> play together. →

3 <u>Be not</u> late for class again. →

4 Andy, <u>doesn't</u> forget your homework. →

5 Let's <u>watching</u> TV. →

6 <u>Don't let's</u> exercise today. →

7 Why don't <u>us</u> play badminton? →

8 How about <u>go</u> to the concert? →

WORDS C take a break 쉬다 traffic light 신호등 icy 얼음으로 덮인 D pot 냄비

15 감탄문, 부가 의문문
Exclamations, Tag questions

1 감탄문

'매우 ~하구나!'라고 자신의 감정, 느낌을 강하게 표현한 문장이다. 명사구의 유무에 따라 What과 How로 시작하고, 문장 끝에 느낌표(!)를 붙인다.

❶ what 감탄문: What + a/an + 형용사 + 명사 + 주어 + 동사!

> She is **a very smart girl.** 그녀는 매우 똑똑한 소녀이다.
>
> **What** a smart girl she is! 그녀는 매우 똑똑한 소녀구나!

❷ how 감탄문: How + 형용사/부사 + 주어 + 동사!

> She is **very smart.** 그녀는 매우 똑똑하다.
>
> **How** smart she is! 그녀는 매우 똑똑하구나!

✎ NOTE 감탄문에서 마지막의 「주어 + 동사」는 생략되기도 한다.

What a smart girl!　　　　　　　　How smart!

2 주의해야 할 감탄문의 형태

❶ what 감탄문에서 형용사의 첫 소리가 모음일 경우에는 부정관사 an을 쓴다.

What *an honest boy* he is!
What *an interesting book* it is!

❷ what 감탄문에서 명사가 복수형이거나 셀 수 없는 경우에는 a/an을 쓰지 않는다.

What *cute puppies* they are!
What *beautiful weather* it is!

❸ 감탄문 마지막에 쓰이는 「주어 + 동사」는 앞에 쓰인 감탄사구와 잘 어울려야 한다.

What a nice garden *they have*!
How well *she dances*!

LET'S CHECK

A 빈칸에 What 또는 How를 넣어 감탄문을 완성하세요.

0   _____What_____ a great idea it is!

1   _____ big the elephant is!

2   _____ an exciting game it was!

3   _____ lucky you are!

4   _____ a pretty girl she is!

5   _____ tall the trees are!

6   _____ tall tress they are!

7   _____ hard he works!

8   _____ fast the horse is running!

9   _____ beautiful eyes she has!

B 우리말과 일치하도록 ( ) 안의 말을 알맞게 배열하세요.

0   그것은 매우 두꺼운 사전이구나! (it, is, thick, a, what, dictionary)
→ _____What a thick dictionary it is!_____

1   그는 농구를 매우 잘 하는구나! (well, he, basketball, plays, how)
→ _____

2   이것은 매우 비싼 시계구나! (expensive, this, is, what, an, watch)
→ _____

3   이 케이크는 정말 맛있구나! (cake, is, this, delicious, how)
→ _____

4   그녀는 매우 긴 머리를 가졌구나! (she, long, what, hair, has)
→ _____

3 부가 의문문

상대방에게 내용을 확인하기 위해 평서문 끝에 덧붙이는 의문문으로, '그렇지?' 또는 '그렇지 않니?'의 의미를 나타낸다. 부가 의문문은 1) 앞 문장이 긍정이면 부정으로, 부정이면 긍정으로 쓰고, 2) 시제는 앞 문장과 일치시킨다. 3) 주어는 앞 문장의 주어에 맞는 인칭대명사를 사용한다.

The book *is* interesting, **isn't it?**

Hippos *can't* jump, **can they?**

The kids *didn't* go to the park, **did they?**

❶ 부정의 부가 의문문

주어 + be동사	*You are* a student, **aren't you**?
주어 + 조동사	*Tom can* play the drums, **can't he**?
주어 + 일반동사	*Sue likes* dogs, **doesn't she**?

❷ 긍정의 부가 의문문

주어 + be동사의 부정형	*You aren't* a student, **are you**?
주어 + 조동사의 부정형	*Tom can't* play the drums, **can he**?
주어 + 일반동사의 부정형	*Sue doesn't* like dogs, **does she**?

❸ 명령문의 부가 의문문: 긍정, 부정에 관계없이 'will you?'를 쓴다.

Close the door, **will you?**

Don't be late, **will you?**

❹ Let's로 시작하는 경우: 긍정, 부정에 관계없이 'shall we?'를 쓴다.

Let's sing together, **shall we?**

Let's not go to the park, **shall we?**

> ✎ NOTE 앞 문장의 주어가 this/that, these/those일 경우, 부가 의문문의 주어는 it이나 they를 쓴다.
>
> *This* is your pen, isn't **this**? [×]
> *This* is your pen, isn't **it**? [○]
>
> *Those* are your puppies, aren't **those**? [×]
> *Those* are your puppies, aren't **they**? [○]

LET'S CHECK

C

( ) 안에서 알맞은 말을 고르세요.

0   Mr. Kim is a nice teacher, isn't (he, Mr. Kim)?

1   This T-shirt is very cheap, (isn't, is) it?

2   James is from England, (is, isn't) he?

3   You can speak French, (can, can't) you?

4   Julie looks like her mother, (isn't, doesn't) she?

5   Tom came alone, (doesn't, didn't) he?

6   This is your coat, (isn't it, isn't this)?

7   Your dog's name is Max, (isn't it, aren't you)?

8   Put the milk in the refrigerator, (will, shall) you?

9   Let's make a snowman, (will, shall) we?

D

주어진 문장의 부가 의문문으로 알맞은 것을 고르세요.

0   You know Mary, _____ⓑ_____   ⓐ isn't it?

1   It is hot today, _____   ⓑ don't you?

2   They are nice people, _____   ⓒ did he?

3   Jim bought a new car, _____   ⓓ won't it?

4   They were at home, _____   ⓔ can't you?

5   Alex didn't do his homework, _____   ⓕ aren't they?

6   You can swim, _____   ⓖ shall we?

7   Clean your room, _____   ⓗ weren't they?

8   Let's walk to the park, _____   ⓘ will you?

9   The game will start soon, _____   ⓙ didn't he?

WORDS   C look like ~을 닮다   alone 혼자   refrigerator 냉장고   snowman 눈사람   D soon 곧

LET'S PRACTICE

A 그림을 보고 what 또는 how와 ( ) 안의 말을 이용하여 감탄문을 완성하세요.

0  1 2  3

0 _____What a long_____ bridge it is! (long)

1 _____ the boy is! (lazy)

2 _____ dinosaur it is! (huge)

3 _____ I am! (happy)

B 다음 문장을 ( ) 안의 말로 시작하는 감탄문으로 바꿔 쓰세요.

0 It is a very helpful lesson. (what)

→ _____What a helpful lesson it is!_____

1 He drives a very big truck. (what)

→ _____

2 The clown looks very funny. (how)

→ _____

3 That is a very old tree. (what)

→ _____

4 You sing very beautifully. (how)

→ _____

WORDS   A lazy 게으른 huge 거대한   B lesson 수업 clown 광대 funny 웃기는, 재미있는

C 빈칸에 알맞은 부가 의문문을 써서 문장을 완성하세요.

0 You have a dog, _____don't you_____?

1 You and I are good friends, _____?

2 Those apples aren't fresh, _____?

3 Dad is sleeping, _____?

4 You can't come to the party, _____?

5 Mrs. Hong doesn't teach English, _____?

6 The man won the contest, _____?

7 We can leave now, _____?

8 Mina, please help me, _____?

9 Let's go swimming, _____?

D 밑줄 친 부분을 바르게 고치세요.

0 <u>How</u> a nice hat you are wearing! → What

1 How lucky <u>are you</u>! →

2 <u>What</u> beautiful the rainbow is! →

3 What <u>a pretty eyes</u> you have! →

4 What <u>a good coffee</u>! →

5 You like music, <u>do you</u>? →

6 This cake is delicious, <u>doesn't it</u>? →

7 These are your crayons, <u>aren't these</u>? →

8 Study hard, <u>will we</u>? →

9 Let's go out, <u>should we</u>? →

STEP 1 **빈칸 완성** ( ) 안의 말을 이용하여 문장을 완성하세요.

1 잠깐만 기다려. (wait)

→ _____ a minute.

2 선생님께 공손해라. (polite)

→ _____ _____ to your teacher.

3 네 여권 잊지 마. (forget)

→ _____ _____ your passport.

4 산책하러 가자. (go)

→ _____ _____ for a walk.

5 피자를 시키는 게 어때? (order)

→ How about _____ pizza?

STEP 2 **어구 배열** 우리말과 일치하도록 ( ) 안의 말을 알맞게 배열하세요.

6 같이 점심 먹자. (have, let's, lunch, together)

→ _____

7 그녀는 매우 사랑스러운 미소를 가졌구나! (a, what, lovely, she, smile, has)

→ _____

8 오늘은 매우 춥구나! (it, cold, today, how, is)

→ _____

9 그 시험은 정말 쉬웠어, 그렇지? (test, wasn't, easy, was, the, it)

→ _____

10 그 게임 너무 많이 하지 마. (that, play, don't, game, too much)

→ _____

영작하기 ( ) 안의 말을 이용하여 우리말을 영어로 옮기세요.

11 다른 사람들에게 친절해라. (kind to, others)

→ _____

12 햇빛에 너무 오래 있지 마. (stay, in the sun, too long)

→ _____

13 박물관 안에서 사진 찍지 마. (take pictures, inside the museum)

→ _____

14 방과 후에 만나자. (meet, after school)

→ _____

15 시간 낭비하지 말자. (waste, time)

→ _____

16 그들은 매우 좋은 이웃들이구나! (nice neighbors)

→ _____

17 이것은 매우 흥미진진한 경기구나! (an exciting game)

→ _____

18 이 마을은 매우 평화롭구나! (peaceful, this town)

→ _____

19 그는 위대한 화가였어, 그렇지 않니? (a great painter)

→ _____

20 그들은 콘서트에 가지 않았어, 그렇지? (go, to the concert)

→ _____

REVIEW TEST
CHAPTER 07

[1-3] 빈칸에 들어갈 말로 알맞은 것을 고르시오.

1

_____ a handsome guy he is!

① Who ② How ③ Why
④ What ⑤ When

2

_____ slowly. You're walking too fast.

① Walks ② Walking
③ Please walk ④ Don't walk
⑤ Let's not walk

3

You are from Korea, _____?

① are you ② do you
③ aren't you ④ don't you
⑤ weren't you

4 두 문장의 뜻이 같도록 할 때 빈칸에 알맞은 것은?

Let's take the elevator.
→ _____ don't we take the elevator?

① Why ② How ③ Let's
④ What ⑤ Where

서술형
[5-6] 빈칸에 알맞은 부가 의문문을 써서 문장을 완성하시오.

5

The man is your father, _____?

6

Your school has a swimming pool, _____?

7 빈칸에 공통으로 들어갈 말은?

· Please _____ make any noise.
· You live in this town, _____ you?

① not ② do ③ are
④ don't ⑤ aren't

8 빈칸에 들어갈 말이 순서대로 바르게 짝지어진 것은?

· Hurry up, _____ we will be late.
· Turn right, _____ you will see the museum.

① or – or ② or – and
③ and – or ④ and – but
⑤ and – and

[9-10] 다음 중 어법상 옳은 문장을 고르시오.

9 ① Please be careful.
  ② Not forget my name.
  ③ Let's studies together.
  ④ Let's don't go to the zoo.
  ⑤ Isn't smoke inside the building.

10 ① How the boy happy is!
  ② What a strange story is it!
  ③ What pretty flowers they are!
  ④ What interesting the movie was!
  ⑤ How wonderful holidays we had!

[11-12] 밑줄 친 부분이 잘못된 것을 고르시오.

11 ① You are tired, <u>aren't you</u>?
  ② The food is delicious, <u>isn't it</u>?
  ③ He was late for school, <u>didn't he</u>?
  ④ She doesn't like seafood, <u>does she</u>?
  ⑤ The snakes aren't dangerous, <u>are they</u>?

12 ① <u>Let's try</u> again.
  ② <u>Wash</u> your face and hands.
  ③ Please wait for me, <u>will you</u>?
  ④ <u>How about going</u> swimming?
  ⑤ <u>Why don't we eating</u> out tonight?

서술형

[13-14] ( ) 안의 말을 알맞게 배열하여 문장을 완성하시오.

13
(a, day, it, what, beautiful, is)

→ _____

14
(the, fish, don't, feed)

→ _____ in the pond.

서술형

[15-16] 우리말과 일치하도록 ( ) 안의 말을 이용하여 문장을 완성하시오.

15
친구들과 싸우지 말자. (let, fight)

→ _____ with our friends.

16
그 역은 정말 가깝구나! (close)

→ _____ the station is!

MEMO

MEMO

MEMO

Your Best Friend on the Way to Becoming a Grammar Master

Grammar
Mate 2

ANSWER KEY

DARAKWON

Grammar Mate 2

〜〜〜〜

ANSWER KEY

CHAPTER 01

Present Continuous
현재진행형

UNIT 01 현재진행형
Present Continuous

LET'S CHECK
p.13, 15

A

1 taking   2 reading   3 sitting   4 watching
5 lying   6 cooking   7 sleeping   8 cleaning
9 writing   10 eating   11 saying   12 smiling
13 dying   14 crying   15 riding   16 singing
17 cutting   18 studying   19 stopping

B

1 is snowing   2 is coming   3 am doing
4 is buying   5 are jumping   6 is tying
7 is putting   8 are playing   9 are running

C

1 isn't[is not] crying   2 aren't[are not] dancing
3 am not listening   4 isn't[is not] sitting
5 isn't[is not] sleeping   6 isn't[is not] running
7 aren't[are not] studying
8 isn't[is not] wearing   9 isn't[is not] cooking

D

1 Are, making   2 Are, enjoying
3 Are, going   4 Is, helping
5 Are, swimming   6 Are, laughing
7 Am, bothering   8 Is, flying
9 Are, waving

LET'S PRACTICE
p.16-17

A

1 meeting   2 drawing   3 putting   4 getting
5 trying   6 buying   7 driving   8 having
9 snowing   10 shopping   11 planning
12 diving   13 stopping   14 speaking
15 raining   16 mixing   17 winning

B

is reading / is lying / are swimming / is playing

C

1 Are, beating   2 Is, setting   3 is throwing

D

1 Are you   2 is not   3 running   4 taking
5 isn't   6 blowing

UNIT 02 현재시제 vs. 현재진행형
Present Simple vs.
Present Continuous

LET'S CHECK
p.19

A

1 (1) goes (2) is going
2 (1) feed (2) am feeding
3 (1) help (2) are helping
4 (1) wears (2) is wearing

B

1 need   2 is drinking   3 Do you know
4 doesn't like   5 is practicing   6 want
7 has   8 are having

LET'S PRACTICE
p.20-21

A

1 at the moment   2 on Fridays
3 once a month   4 right now   5 today

B

1 isn't   2 Is   3 don't   4 aren't   5 doesn't
6 isn't   7 Are   8 is   9 Do

C

1 is sleeping   2 are jumping   3 plays
4 eat   5 is snowing   6 doesn't[does not] like
7 don't[do not] believe   8 isn't[is not] working
9 gets up

D

1 Do you believe   2 is drinking   3 likes
4 I love   5 washing   6 is knocking
7 meet   8 is not   9 Are

LET'S WRITE
p.22-23

STEP 1

1 are sitting   2 is fixing   3 am not doing
4 is pouring   5 Are you reading

6 I am looking out the window.

7 Sally is shopping on the Internet.

8 Tom is not cleaning his room.

9 Is Jessica talking on the phone

10 Is the doorbell ringing?

11 We are walking on the beach.

12 They are painting the ceiling.

13 She is cutting her fingernails.

14 People are lying on the grass.

15 You aren't[are not] telling the truth.

16 They aren't[are not] eating at a restaurant.

17 He isn't[is not] wearing a tie

18 Is the water boiling?

19 Am I walking too fast?

20 Are you asking me?

REVIEW TEST
p.24-25

1 ⑤ 2 ⑤ 3 is buying 4 aren't doing
5 Are you using 6 ④ 7 ④ 8 ① 9 ⑤
10 ⑤ 11 ② 12 ④ 13 ② 14 ④
15 are crossing 16 loves 17 Is he lying

해설

1 〈단모음 + 단자음〉으로 끝나는 동사는 자음을 한번 더 쓰고 -ing를 붙인다. ⑤ swim – swimming

2 -y로 끝나는 동사는 그대로 -ing를 붙인다.
⑤ study – studying

3 현재진행형은 「be동사의 현재형 + 동사원형-ing」이 다.

4 현재진행형 부정문은 「be동사의 현재형 + not + 동사 원형-ing」이다. are not은 aren't로 줄여 쓸 수 있다.

5 현재진행형 의문문은 「be동사의 현재형 + 주어 + 동 사원형-ing?」이다.

6 ①②③⑤는 주어가 복수이므로 are가 알맞고, ④는 주 어가 단수(Ann)이므로 is가 알맞다.

7 현재진행형 부정문은 「be동사의 현재형 + not + 동사 원형-ing」이다.

8 know는 상태 동사이므로 현재진행형을 쓰지 않고 현 재시제를 쓴다.

9 현재진행형과 가장 어울리는 시간 표현은 ⑤ at the moment(지금은)이다.

10 반복적인 습관은 현재시제, 지금 하고 있는 일은 현재 진행형으로 나타낸다.

11 상대방에게 지금 도서관에 가고 있는지를 묻고 있다. 현재진행형으로 묻고 답해야 하므로 각 빈칸에 알맞 은 be동사는 ② Are – am이다.

12 want는 상태 동사이므로 현재진행형을 쓰지 않고 현 재시제를 쓴다. ④ am wanting → want

13 right now는 현재진행형과 어울리는 시간 표현이다.
② check → am checking

14 지금 전철역을 찾고 있으므로 현재진행형을 사용한 다. 주어가 I이므로 ④ am looking for가 알맞다.

15 현재진행형은 「be동사의 현재형 + 동사원형-ing」이 다. 주어가 Two boys이므로 be동사는 are를 쓴다.

16 love는 상태 동사이므로 현재진행형을 쓰지 않고 현 재시제를 쓴다. 주어가 3인칭 단수(My sister)이므로 loves가 알맞다.

17 현재진행형 의문문은 「be동사의 현재형 + 주어 + 동 사원형-ing?」이고, -ie로 끝나는 동사는 ie를 y로 고 치고 -ing를 붙인다. (lie → lying)

CHAPTER
02

Past Simple
과거시제

UNIT 03 Be동사의 과거형
Past Simple: *Be*

LET'S CHECK
p.29

A

1 wasn't 2 wasn't 3 were 4 was
5 was 6 were 7 were 8 weren't
9 wasn't

B

1 Was / he was 2 Was / it wasn't
3 Were / they weren't 4 Were / they were
5 Was / it wasn't 6 Was / he was
7 Were / I wasn't 8 Was / it was

LET'S PRACTICE
p.30-31

A

1 is 2 was 3 was 4 is 5 was

6 is 7 were 8 was, was 9 were, are

B

1 was, wasn't 2 weren't, were

3 was, wasn't

C

1 Alex was born in London.
2 This song wasn't[was not] popular.
3 The trees weren't[were not] tall.
4 There were some books on the desk.

D

1 Was he / he was 2 Were they / they were
3 Were Bill and Sue / they weren't
4 Was it / it was

UNIT 04 일반동사의 과거형 1
Past Simple 1

LET'S CHECK
p.33, 35

A

1 jumped 2 finished 3 laughed
4 watched 5 liked 6 danced 7 smiled
8 cried 9 tried 10 carried 11 played
12 stayed 13 enjoyed 14 stopped
15 dropped 16 planned 17 passed
18 wanted 19 shouted

B

1 (1) rains (2) rained 2 (1) study (2) studied
3 (1) arrives (2) arrived 4 (1) visit (2) visited

C

1 did 2 ate 3 got 4 went 5 had
6 put 7 saw 8 sat 9 slept 10 wrote
11 bought 12 caught 13 drank 14 drove
15 read 16 rode 17 ran 18 taught
19 broke

D

1 leave 2 meet 3 ring 4 send 5 sing
6 take 7 feel 8 wear 9 become 10 cut
11 fall 12 hit 13 know 14 build
15 make 16 sell 17 swim 18 lose
19 win

LET'S WRITE
p.36-37

A

1 gets 2 rose 3 study 4 felt 5 wrote
6 cooked 7 every day 8 last night
9 on Sundays

B

1 Janet wore a lovely hat
2 My mother drove me to school
3 My uncle had two dogs
4 The train left

C

1 won 2 swam 3 dropped 4 changed
5 became 6 bought 7 fell, cried

D

heard / walked / saw / shouted / ran / called /
caught

UNIT 05 일반동사의 과거형 2
Past Simple 2

LET'S CHECK
p.39

A

1 didn't go 2 didn't finish 3 didn't like
4 didn't ring

B

1 Did, teach 2 Did, pass 3 Did, find
4 Did, go

LET'S WRITE
p.40-41

A

1 enjoyed 2 didn't 3 feel 4 drank
5 didn't 6 fell 7 had 8 didn't

B

1 (1) She didn't lose her car key yesterday.
  (2) Did she lose her car key yesterday?
2 (1) They didn't move to a new house.
  (2) Did they move to a new house?
3 (1) The school bus didn't arrive on time.
  (2) Did the school bus arrive on time?

C

1 Did, break / he did 2 Did, walk / I didn't
3 Did, open / it didn't

D

1 like 2 Did 3 Did 4 get 5 didn't

LET'S WRITE

p.42-43

STEP 1

1 was 2 were 3 wasn't 4 weren't
5 Were

STEP 2

6 She bought a new car
7 Their son became an actor.
8 Did you come home by taxi?
9 We didn't meet him
10 Did Paul take these pictures?

STEP 3

11 We were in the sixth grade last year.
12 We went camping last weekend.
13 She cut the cake in half.
14 They drank tea after lunch.
15 The weather wasn't[was not] good
   yesterday.
16 She didn't[did not] read my message.
17 We didn't[did not] stay at the hotel.
18 Was she late for school yesterday?
19 Did you sleep well last night?
20 Did you see the singer yesterday?

REVIEW TEST

p.44-45

1 ⑤ 2 ④ 3 ② 4 ④ 5 ② 6 ③
7 ② 8 ① 9 ③ 10 ② 11 it wasn't
12 they did 13 ③ 14 ⑤
15 He was a famous actor
16 Ryan dropped his new smartphone
17 Did you put this box

해설

1 〈단모음 + 단자음〉으로 끝나는 동사는 자음을 한번 더 쓰고 -ed를 붙인다. ⑤ plan – planned

2 ④ hit은 현재형과 과거형의 형태가 같다.

3 yesterday는 과거를 나타내고 주어가 단수(Jenny)이 므로 ② was가 알맞다. ⑤ didn't 뒤에는 동사원형이 와야 하므로 형용사 angry 앞에는 쓸 수 없다.

4 last night은 과거를 나타내므로 ④ didn't study가 알맞다. ⑤ wasn't 뒤에는 동사를 쓸 수 없다.

5 yesterday는 과거를 나타내므로 run의 과거형인 ② ran이 알맞다. ⑤의 didn't 뒤에는 동사원형을 써야 하 므로 didn't run으로 써야 알맞다.

6 ①②④⑤는 was, ③은 are의 과거형인 were가 알맞 다.

7 두 문장 모두 빈칸 뒤에 동사원형이 쓰였고 과거를 나 타내는 부사(구)가 쓰였으므로 ② did가 알맞다. ④⑤ 뒤에는 동사가 올 수 없다.

8 was가 쓰였으므로 '지금'을 뜻하는 ① now는 알맞지 않다.

9 일반동사 과거형의 부정문은 「did not[didn't] + 동사 원형」이다.

10 일반동사 과거형의 의문문은 「Did + 주어 + 동사원 형?」이다.

11 Was로 묻고 주어가 the book이므로, 대답은 it을 주 어로 써서 No, it wasn't로 한다.

12 Did로 묻고 주어가 Paul and Jane이므로, 대답은 they를 주어로 써서 Yes, they did로 한다.

13 ③ last month는 과거를 나타내므로 buy의 과거형 인 bought를 써야 알맞다.

14 ⑤ two years ago는 과거를 나타내므로 are의 과거 형인 were를 써야 알맞다.

15 주어가 He이고 과거에 '~였다'의 의미이므로 is의 과거형인 was를 써서 나타낸다.

16 〈단모음 + 단자음〉으로 끝나는 동사는 자음을 한번 더 쓰고 -ed를 붙인다. (drop → dropped)

17 일반동사 과거형의 의문문은 「Did + 주어 + 동사원 형?」이다.

CHAPTER 03

Future Time
미래 표현

UNIT 06 미래 표현 1: Will
Future Time 1: *Will*

LET'S CHECK

p.49

A

1 won't 2 won't 3 will 4 won't 5 will

6 will 7 won't 8 won't 9 won't

B

1 Will, join 2 Will, do 3 Will, go

4 Will, be

LET'S PRACTICE

p.50-51

A

1 will visit 2 will be 3 will miss 4 will do

5 will write 6 will sell 7 will rise

B

1 will be 2 will live 3 will come

4 won't[will not] leave 5 won't[will not] like

6 Will you be 7 Will Tina eat

C

1 Will, do / I will 2 Will, win / she won't

3 Will, leave / he won't

D

1 be 2 close 3 won't 4 have

5 Will you 6 will not

UNIT 07 미래 표현 2: Be going to
Future Time 2: *Be going to*

LET'S CHECK

p.53

A

1 are 2 are going to 3 study 4 going to

5 Are 6 to arrive 7 aren't 8 Are 9 have

B

1 are going to get 2 am going to cook

3 are going to take 4 is going to see

5 aren't[are not] going to travel

6 isn't[is not] going to start

7 Is he going to buy

8 Are you going to study

9 Are we going to wait

LET'S WRITE

p.54-55

A

1 is going to rain 2 is going to mail

3 is going to eat 4 are going to take

5 is going to buy

B

1 isn't[is not] going to exercise

2 am going to wash

3 are going to study

4 is going to drink

5 isn't[is not] going to change

6 am not going to buy

7 is going to be

8 is going to wear

9 am going to call

C

1 Are, going to take / they aren't

2 Are, going to paint / they are

3 Is, going to wear / he isn't

LET'S WRITE

p.56-57

STEP **1**

1 will be 2 are going to meet

3 won't tell 4 Are you going to join

5 aren't going to travel

STEP **2**

6 We will do our best.

7 He won't listen to me.

8 Will you go to the concert

9 I am going to learn Chinese

10 He is not going to quit his job.

STEP **3**

11 People will travel into space

12 We will wait for him until 7 o'clock.

13 I will carry the suitcase for you.

14 I won't[will not] give up.

15 Will they arrive on time?

16 We are going to miss the school bus.

17 We are going to go on a field trip to the museum.

18 My brother is going to study law at university.

19 Susan isn't[is not] going to drink coffee this morning.

20 Is he going to give a speech tonight?

REVIEW TEST

p.58-59

1 am going to 2 is not going to
3 Are you going to 4 ⑤ 5 ③ 6 ②
7 ④ 8 ⑤ 9 ② 10 ② 11 ④
12 runs → run 13 is → are
14 am going to ride 15 won't[will not] lose
16 Are they going to help

해설

1 「will + 동사원형」은 「be going to + 동사원형」으로 바꿔 쓸 수 있다. 주어가 I이므로 am going to가 알맞다.

2 will not은 be not going to로 바꿔 쓸 수 있다. 주어가 Jeff이므로 is not going to가 알맞다.

3 be going to의 의문문은 「Be동사 + 주어 + going to + 동사원형?」이다. 주어가 you이므로 Are you going to가 알맞다.

4 will 뒤에는 동사원형이 와야 하므로 ①②③④는 알맞지 않다. will의 부정문은 「will not[won't] + 동사원형」 형태이므로 ⑤는 맞는 문장이다.

5 미래의 일을 나타내는 의문문은 「Will + 주어 + 동사원형?」 또는 「Be동사 + 주어 + going to + 동사원형?」으로 나타낼 수 있다. ④⑤처럼 will과 going to는 함께 쓰지 않는다.

6 will의 부정문은 「will not[won't] + 동사원형」이다.

7 ①②③⑤는 「be going to + 동사원형」 형태로 쓰여 '~할 것이다, ~할 예정이다'의 의미이다. ④는 to 뒤에 명사가 쓰여 '~에 가고 있다'는 현재진행형의 의미이다.

8 두 문장 모두 be동사가 쓰였으므로 「be going to + 동사원형」 구문이 올 수 있다.

9 going to 앞에는 be동사(Is), 동사원형(take) 앞에는 will이 올 수 있다. 내용상 우산을 가져가겠다고 해야 자연스러우므로 ③ won't는 알맞지 않다.

10 ① won't not → won't, ③ Will → Are, ④ Are → Is, ⑤ sleeping → sleep으로 고쳐야 알맞다.

11 ④ 어제의 일을 묻고 있으므로 과거형을 써서 Did you meet him yesterday?으로 물어야 한다.

12 will 뒤에는 동사원형이 와야 하므로 runs는 run으로 고쳐야 알맞다.

13 Sumi and Jane은 복수이므로 is는 are로 고쳐야 알맞다.

14 주어가 I이므로 am going to ride로 나타낸다.

15 will의 부정문은 「will not[won't] + 동사원형」이다.

16 be going to의 의문문은 「Be동사 + 주어 + going to + 동사원형?」이다. 주어가 they이므로 Are they going to help가 알맞다.

CHAPTER
04

Modal Verbs
조동사

UNIT 08 Can, May
Can, May

LET'S CHECK

p.63, 65

A
1 go 2 Can 3 fly 4 cannot use 5 play
6 Can he 7 answer 8 cannot 9 can't

B
1 can't 2 can 3 can't 4 can 5 can
6 can 7 can't 8 can 9 can't

C
1 may not 2 may 3 may not 4 may
5 may not 6 may not 7 may 8 may

D
1 ⓑ 2 ⓒ 3 ⓑ 4 ⓐ 5 ⓒ 6 ⓑ
7 ⓐ 8 ⓒ

LET'S PRACTICE

p.66-67

A
1 can't change 2 can design 3 can't float

B
1 have a test 2 be late 3 be cold
4 break it 5 have the wrong address

C
1 Stella can speak two languages.
2 Jack may not be in his office.
3 I can't remember his name.
4 You may borrow my car.

D

1 We can't go hiking today.
2 This may be Dave's cellphone.
3 Can I close the window?
4 You may keep the change.

UNIT 09 Should, Must, Have to
Should, Must, Have to

LET'S CHECK

p.69, 71

A

1 shouldn't 2 shouldn't 3 should
4 shouldn't 5 shouldn't 6 shouldn't
7 should 8 should 9 shouldn't

B

1 must not 2 must 3 must 4 must not
5 must 6 must 7 must not 8 must
9 must not

C

1 has to 2 have to 3 has to 4 have to
5 has to 6 have to 7 has to 8 has to
9 have to

D

1 don't have to 2 don't have to
3 doesn't have to 4 don't have to
5 don't have to 6 don't have to
7 doesn't have to 8 doesn't have to
9 don't have to

LET'S PRACTICE

p.72-73

A

1 shouldn't go 2 shouldn't drink
3 should leave 4 shouldn't go
5 shouldn't stay 6 should put
7 shouldn't eat 8 should drive
9 should be

B

1 must wear 2 must not bring 3 must be

C

1 shouldn't 2 must not 3 doesn't have to
4 should 5 shouldn't 6 should
7 don't have to 8 has to 9 have to

D

1 finish 2 don't have to 3 have to
4 don't have to 5 swim 6 must not speak
7 water 8 must 9 has to

LET'S WRITE

p.74-75

STEP 1

1 can use 2 can't[cannot] live
3 Can[May] I ask 4 may not be 5 may go

STEP 2

6 You must not go there alone.
7 Sally has to take care of her brother.
8 Everyone must follow the rules.
9 Students don't have to bring their lunch.
10 You should eat more vegetables.

STEP 3

11 Can you play a musical instrument?
12 He may be Ann's boyfriend.
13 He may not agree with your plan.
14 Can[May] I use this printer?
15 Can you close the curtains?
16 You must[have to] dry-clean this shirt.
17 She must[has to] get off at the next stop.
18 You must not believe him.
19 We don't have to buy the tickets.
20 You should do your best for this exam.

REVIEW TEST

p.76-77

1 ③ 2 ③ 3 ③ 4 ④ 5 ①
6 has to keep 7 ② 8 ④ 9 ② 10 ②
11 ④ 12 ③ 13 shouldn't[should not]
14 don't have to 15 may 16 have to
17 must not

해설

1 '~할 수 없다'는 ③ cannot[can't]을 사용한다.

2 '~해야 한다, ~하는 것이 좋겠다'는 ③ should를 사용한다. 주어가 I이므로 ④ has to는 알맞지 않다.

3 can 뒤에는 동사원형이 와야 하므로 ③ swims well은 알맞지 않다.

4 ①②③⑤는 '~일지도 모른다'는 약한 추측, ④는 '~해도 좋다'는 허가의 뜻으로 쓰였다.

5 be good at은 '~을 잘한다'의 의미이므로 ① '그녀는

6 '~해야 한다'는 뜻의 must는 have/has to로 바꿔 쓸
　수 있다. 주어가 3인칭 단수(He)이므로 has to keep
　이 알맞다.

7 '~이 아닐지도 모른다'는 약한 추측은 may not을 사
　용한다.

8 상대방에게 '~해주시겠습니까?'라고 요청할 때는
　「Would/Could/Will/Can you + 동사원형?」으로 나
　타낸다.

9 가방을 잃어버렸다는 상대방에게 분실물 보관소에 가
　보라고 조언하는 내용이므로, '~해야 한다, ~하는 것
　이 좋겠다'는 의미의 ② should를 쓰는 것이 자연스럽
　다.

10 '~일지도 모른다'는 약한 추측은 ② may를 사용한
　다.

11 Can으로 물었으므로 ④는 No, you can't로 대답해
　야 알맞다.

12 ③ 조동사 must 뒤에는 동사원형인 clean이 와야 한
　다.

13 should의 부정형은 shouldn't[should not]이다.

14 '~할 필요가 없다'는 don't/doesn't have to를 사
　용한다.

15 '~일지도 모른다'는 약한 추측은 may를 사용한다.

16 '~해야 한다'는 must나 have/has to를 사용한다.

17 '~해서는 안 된다'는 금지의 뜻은 must not을 써서
　나타낸다.

CHAPTER 05

Interrogatives
의문사

UNIT 10 의문사 1
Interrogatives 1

LET'S CHECK
p.81, 83

A
1 Who(m)　2 Whose　3 Who　4 Who(m)

---

5 Whose　6 Who　7 Whose　8 Who
9 Who(m)

B
1 Who　2 Who(m)　3 Whose　4 Who
5 Whose　6 Who　7 Who(m)　8 Who(m)
9 Whose

C
1 Which　2 What　3 What　4 Which
5 What　6 Which　7 What　8 Which

D
1 Which dish　2 What kind
3 Which color　4 What size

LET'S PRACTICE
p.84-85

A
1 What　2 What　3 Which　4 Whose
5 Which　6 Whose　7 What　8 Who

B
1 Who　2 Which　3 Whose　4 Which
5 What

C
1 Who can　2 What did you
3 Whose gloves　4 Which do you

D
1 do you live with
2 friends are they
3 subject do you like
4 seat is hers

UNIT 11 의문사 2
Interrogatives 2

LET'S CHECK
p.87, 89

A
1 When　2 When　3 Where　4 Why
5 Why　6 When　7 When　8 Why
9 Where

B
1 Where　2 Why　3 Where　4 When

C
1 ⓕ　2 ⓓ　3 ⓑ　4 ⓖ　5 ⓒ　6 ⓗ　7 ⓔ

D

1 How much 2 How many 3 How many
4 How much 5 How many 6 How much
7 How many 8 How much 9 How many

LET'S PRACTICE

p.90-91

A

1 When 2 How 3 Why 4 How far
5 long 6 often 7 tall 8 much 9 many

B

1 How many 2 How far 3 How much

C

1 © 2 ① 3 ⑨ 4 ⓓ 5 ⓐ
6 ⓗ 7 ⓔ 8 ① 9 ⓑ

D

1 What time 2 Why 3 What day
4 What

LET'S WRITE

p.92-93

STEP 1

1 Who 2 What 3 Whose 4 Which
5 How

STEP 2

6 What will happen next?
7 What does this word mean?
8 How far can you jump?
9 How often do you go swimming?
10 Where do you keep your pictures?

STEP 3

11 What day is it today?
12 Who is the captain of the team?
13 What do you want for Christmas?
14 Where are they going?
15 How old is your sister?
16 How long is the Han River?
17 When did you finish your homework?
18 Why did they leave early?
19 How much money do you spend in a
   month?
20 How many hours did you sleep last night?

REVIEW TEST

p.94-95

1 ③ 2 ⑤ 3 ③ 4 When 5 Where
6 Who 7 Why 8 ③ 9 ⑤ 10 ③
11 ⑤ 12 ⑤ 13 How tall is this building?
14 What kind of music do you like?
15 What subject 16 Whose key
17 How far

해설

1 저녁으로 '무엇(What)'을 먹었는지 묻고 있다.

2 정해진 대상 중에서 '어느(Which)' 고양이가 상대방의 것인지 묻고 있다.

3 교통수단은 ③ How로 묻는다.

4 What time(몇 시)은 When(언제)으로 바꿔 쓸 수 있다.

5 여동생이 '어디에(Where)' 있는지 묻고 있다.

6 '누가(Who)' 화분을 깼는지 묻고 있다.

7 이유는 Why(왜)로 묻는다.

8 ①②④⑤는 How(어떤, 어떻게), ③은 What(무엇)이 알맞다.

9 첫 번째 문장은 ①②⑤, 두 번째 문장은 ⑤만 가능하다.

10 ① 의문사 의문문은 Yes/No로 대답할 수 없다. ② '너는 쇼핑몰에 어떻게 가니?' ③ '너희 어머니는 무슨 일을 하시니?' ④ '그녀는 커피를 얼마나 자주 마시니?' ⑤ '중국의 만리장성은 얼마나 깁니까?'

11 ⑤ 이름을 물을 때는 What(무엇)을 사용한다.

12 ⑤ '몇 번'인지 횟수를 물을 때는 How many times 로 묻는다.

13 be동사가 있는 문장은 「의문사 + be동사 + 주어 ~?」 형태로 쓴다.

14 '어떤 종류의 ~'는 「What kind of + 명사」로 나타내고, 뒤에는 의문문 어순을 따른다.

15 '무슨 ~'은 「What + 명사」로 묻는다.

16 '누구의 ~'는 「Whose + 명사」로 묻는다.

17 거리는 How far로 묻는다.

CHAPTER
06

Comparisons
비교

UNIT 12 비교급
Comparatives

LET'S CHECK
p.99

A

1 smaller 2 bigger 3 more famous
4 easier 5 more difficult 6 longer
7 busier 8 sweeter 9 hotter 10 cheaper
11 more expensive 12 warmer 13 colder
14 higher 15 luckier 16 better 17 worse
18 more 19 less

B

1 larger 2 prettier 3 thinner
4 more comfortable 5 better
6 more beautifully 7 more safely
8 earlier 9 worse

LET'S PRACTICE
p.100-101

A

1 smaller than 2 longer than
3 thicker than

B

1 Oranges are sweeter than lemons.
2 Gold is more expensive than silver.
3 Egypt is hotter than Korea.
4 Snails move more slowly than turtles.

C

1 earlier 2 wider 3 more 4 better
5 younger 6 happier 7 more popular
8 mine 9 do

D

1 more 2 worse 3 less 4 more

UNIT 13 최상급
Superlatives

LET'S CHECK
p.103

A

1 hardest 2 biggest 3 most famous
4 easiest 5 smallest 6 most beautiful
7 prettiest 8 smartest 9 hottest
10 coldest 11 highest 12 funniest
13 cheapest 14 most delicious 15 deepest
16 busiest 17 best 18 most 19 least

B

1 shortest 2 strongest 3 latest
4 thinnest 5 happiest 6 most difficult
9 worst

LET'S PRACTICE
p.104-05

A

1 the cheapest 2 the nicest 3 the best
4 the happiest 5 the tallest
6 the most exciting 7 the worst
8 the funniest 9 The longest

B

1 the biggest 2 the shortest
3 the most expensive

C

1 oldest 2 cleverer 3 cleverest 4 most
5 best 6 less 7 easier 8 busiest
9 more

D

1 better 2 than 3 bigger 4 the best
5 most wonderful 6 nicest 7 most
8 fastest 9 the oldest

LET'S WRITE
p.106-107

STEP 1

1 colder than 2 thinner than 3 the longest
4 the most popular 5 harder than

STEP 2

6 An airplane is faster than a train.
7 She has more free time than me.
8 is much more dangerous than a cat.
9 History is the most interesting subject
10 It is the best idea of the year.

11 The sun is brighter than the moon.

12 My father is busier than my mother.

13 Bill is more diligent than Mike.

14 This website is more helpful than that book.

15 It is the oldest computer in the office.

16 Julie is the prettiest girl in the class.

17 The science test was the most difficult of all the tests.

18 He was the greatest inventor in history.

19 He is the best swimmer in Korea.

20 I got the worst score in math.

REVIEW TEST

p.109-110

1 ⑤   2 ②   3 ③   4 earlier
5 more expensive   6 ④   7 ③   8 ②
9 ③   10 shorter than   11 the longest
12 ④   13 more well → better
14 stronger → strongest
15 more diligent than   16 worse than
17 the coldest month

해설

1 2음절 이상이면 more, most를 붙인다. ⑤ famous – more famous – most famous

2 than 앞에는 비교급이 와야 하므로 soft의 비교급인 ② softer가 알맞다.

3 the 뒤에는 최상급이 와야 하므로 fast의 최상급인 ③ fastest가 알맞다.

4 아버지가 1시간 더 일찍 일어났으므로 early의 비교급인 earlier를 써야 알맞다.

5 장갑이 5,000원 더 비싸므로 expensive의 비교급인 more expensive를 써야 알맞다.

6 '~보다 더 …한'은 「비교급(thicker) + than」으로 나타낸다. 비교의 대상이 '내 것'이므로 mine을 쓴다.

7 than 앞에는 비교급(prettier), the 뒤에는 최상급(smartest)이 와야 한다.

8 '훨씬 더 ~한'은 「much/still/far/even/a lot + 비교급」으로 나타낸다. ② very는 비교급 앞에 쓸 수 없다.

9 Judy는 47kg이고 Tom은 55kg이므로 ③은 일치하지 않는다.

10 *Toy Story* 4의 상영시간이 *The Lion King*보다 더 짧으므로 「비교급 + than」 구문을 이용해 shorter than을 쓴다.

11 *Aladdin*의 상영시간이 셋 중 가장 길기 때문에 「the + 최상급」 구문을 이용해 the longest를 쓴다.

12 ④ clean의 비교급은 cleaner이다.

13 well의 비교급은 better이다.

14 '~ 중에 가장 …한'은 「the + 최상급(strongest)」으로 나타낸다.

15 '~보다 더 …한'은 「비교급(more diligent) + than」으로 나타낸다.

16 bad의 비교급은 worse이므로 worse than이 알맞다.

17 '가장 추운 달'은 cold의 최상급을 써서 the coldest month로 나타낸다.

CHAPTER 07

Types of Sentences
문장의 종류

UNIT 14 명령문, 제안문
Imperatives, Suggestions

LET'S CHECK

p.113

A
1 Put   2 feed   3 Be   4 jump   5 wake

B
1 Let's   2 Let's not   3 Let's   4 Let's not
5 Let's not   6 Let's   7 Let's

LET'S PRACTICE

p.114-115

A
1 Turn   2 wait   3 be   4 Don't read   5 Call
6 get   7 Don't park   8 help   9 Don't make

B
1 or   2 and   3 or   4 and   5 or   6 or
7 and

C

1 cross the road 2 cook something
3 wash them 4 have a party 5 drive softly

D

1 Be careful 2 Let's 3 Don't be 4 don't
5 watch 5 Let's not 6 we 7 going

UNIT 15 감탄문, 부가 의문문
Exclamations, Tag questions

LET'S CHECK
p.117, 119

A

1 How 2 What 3 How 4 What 5 How
6 What 7 How 8 How 9 What

B

1 How well he plays basketball!
2 What an expensive watch this is!
3 How delicious this cake is!
4 What long hair she has!

C

1 isn't 2 isn't 3 can't 4 doesn't
5 didn't 6 isn't it 7 isn't it 8 will 9 shall

D

1 ⓐ 2 ⓕ 3 ⓙ 4 ⓗ 5 ⓒ
6 ⓔ 7 ⓘ 8 ⓖ 9 ⓓ

LET'S PRACTICE
p.120-121

A

1 How lazy 2 What a huge 3 How happy

B

1 What a big truck he drives!
2 How funny the clown looks!
3 What an old tree that is!
4 How beautifully you sing!

C

1 aren't we 2 are they 3 isn't he
4 can you 5 does she 6 didn't he
7 can't we 8 will you 9 shall we

D

1 you are 2 How 3 pretty eyes
4 good coffee 5 don't you 6 isn't it
7 aren't they 8 will you 9 shall we

LET'S WRITE
p.122-123

STEP 1

1 Wait 2 Be polite 3 Don't forget
4 Let's go 5 ordering

STEP 2

6 Let's have lunch together.
7 What a lovely smile she has!
8 How cold it is today!
9 The test was easy, wasn't it?
10 Don't play that game too much.

STEP 3

11 Be kind to others.
12 Don't stay in the sun too long.
13 Don't take pictures inside the museum.
14 Let's meet after school.
15 Let's not waste time.
16 What nice neighbors they are!
17 What an exciting game this is!
18 How peaceful this town is!
19 He was a great painter, wasn't he?
20 They didn't go to the concert, did they?

REVIEW TEST
p.124-125

1 ④ 2 ③ 3 ③ 4 ① 5 isn't he
6 doesn't it 7 ④ 8 ② 9 ① 10 ③
11 ③ 12 ⑤
13 What a beautiful day it is!
14 Don't feed the fish 15 Let's not fight
16 How close

해설

1 명사구 a handsome guy를 강조하는 감탄문이므로 ④ What으로 시작한다.

2 너무 빨리 걷는다고 했으므로 '천천히 걸어라'의 의미가 적절하다. 긍정 명령문은 동사원형으로 시작하고, 명령문 앞, 뒤에는 please를 붙일 수 있다.

3 You are로 시작하므로 부가 의문문은 ③ aren't you?가 알맞다.

4 「Let's + 동사원형」과 비슷한 표현으로는 「Why don't we + 동사원형?」과 「How about + 동사원형-ing?」가 있다.

5 The man is로 시작하므로 부가 의문문은 isn't he?가 알맞다.

6 Your school has로 시작하므로 부가 의문문은

doesn't it?이 알맞다.

7 부정 명령문은 동사원형 앞에 don't를 쓴다. You live로 시작하는 문장의 부가 의문문은 don't you?가 알맞다.

8 '~해라, 그러면 …할 것이다'는 「명령문 + and」, '~해라, 그렇지 않으면 …할 것이다'는 「명령문 + or」로 나타낸다.

9 ② Not → Don't, ③ Let's studies → Let's study, ④ Let's don't → Let's not, ⑤ Isn't → Don't로 고쳐야 알맞다.

10 ① How the boy happy is! → How happy the boy is!, ② is it → it is, ④ What → How, ⑤ How → What으로 고쳐야 알맞다.

11 ③ He was로 시작하므로 부가 의문문은 wasn't he?가 알맞다.

12 '~하는 것이 어때?'는 「Why don't we + 동사원형?」 또는 「How about + 동사원형-ing?」로 나타낸다. 따라서 ⑤ eating → eat으로 고쳐야 알맞다.

13 What으로 시작하는 감탄문은 「What + a/an + 형용사 + 명사 + 주어 + 동사!」 형태로 쓴다.

14 부정 명령문은 「Don't + 동사원형」 형태이다.

15 '~하지 말자'는 「Let's not + 동사원형」 형태이다.

16 형용사 close를 강조하는 감탄문이므로 How로 시작한다.

WORKBOOK

UNIT 01 현재진행형
Present Continuous

p.4-5

Ⓐ
1 is sleeping   2 isn't[is not] doing
3 isn't[is not] singing   4 is wearing
5 are shaking   6 isn't[is not] washing
7 isn't[is not] eating   8 are studying
9 aren't[are not] sitting

Ⓑ
1 Are, lying   2 Are, swimming   3 Is, snowing

Ⓒ
1 shaving   2 cutting   3 running
4 speaking   5 is not   6 are   7 Are they
8 reading   9 Are

Ⓓ
1 Are you waiting   2 is getting   3 are dying
4 isn't[is not] paying

UNIT 02 현재시제 vs. 현재진행형
Present Simple vs.
Present Continuous

p.6-7

Ⓐ
1 (1) right now (2) once a month
2 (1) often (2) at the moment

Ⓑ
1 study   2 is playing   3 gets   4 speak
5 is eating   6 has   7 love   8 are riding
9 wears

Ⓒ
1 don't   2 Do   3 isn't   4 Does   5 doesn't
6 are   7 running   8 don't   9 isn't

Ⓓ
1 wants   2 Are you cleaning
3 isn't[is not] using   4 are having

UNIT 03 Be동사의 과거형
Past Simple: Be

p.8-9

Ⓐ
1 wasn't   2 were   3 wasn't   4 Were
5 were   6 were   7 was   8 Was   9 weren't

Ⓑ
1 Were they / they weren't
2 Were you / I was
3 Was your mother / she was
4 Was the food / it wasn't

C

1 was 2 are 3 Were 4 Is 5 was
6 was 7 is

D

1 The eggs weren't[were not]
2 Was the math test
3 Were you
4 We weren't[were not]

C

1 Did she call 119 this morning?
2 I didn't[did not] meet my friend last weekend.
3 Did they study for a test last week?
4 You didn't[did not] wash the dishes after dinner.

D

1 didn't[did not] take 2 Did you bring
3 Did Amy and Ted join 4 didn't[did not] start

UNIT 04 일반동사의 과거형 1
Past Simple 1

p.10-11

A

1 helped 2 closed 3 arrived 4 studied
5 tried 6 played 7 stopped 8 dropped
9 planned 10 came 11 built 12 caught
13 did 14 ate 15 heard 16 left
17 made 18 ran 19 wrote

B

1 (1) cry (2) cried 2 (1) go (2) went
3 (1) meet (2) met 4 (1) reads (2) read

C

1 called 2 ate 3 set 4 taught 5 bought
6 swam 7 carried 8 saw 9 passed

D

1 lived 2 drove 3 stopped 4 made

UNIT 05 일반동사의 과거형 2
Past Simple 2

p.12-13

A

1 didn't see 2 didn't hear 3 didn't eat
4 didn't start 5 didn't sleep 6 didn't do
7 didn't bring 8 didn't come 9 didn't leave

B

1 Did, fall / it didn't 2 Did, lose / she did
3 Did, send / he did 4 Did, go / they didn't

UNIT 06 미래 표현 1: Will
Future Time 1: *Will*

p.14-15

A

1 will be 2 Will 3 go 4 be 5 have
6 won't 7 they finish 8 arrive 9 will get

B

1 will leave 2 won't[will not] be
3 won't[will not] go 4 Will, invite
5 will work 6 won't[will not] buy
7 won't[will not] forgive
8 Will, be 9 Will, join

C

1 will make 2 will do 3 will buy

D

1 will answer 2 won't[will not] go
3 will be 4 Will they pass

UNIT 07 미래 표현 2: Be going to
Future Time 2: *Be going to*

p.16-17

A

1 is going to wear 2 am going to skip
3 is going to call 4 are going to go
5 is going to buy 6 am going to stay
7 is going to find

B

1 Their new album is going to be
2 We are not going to go
3 Are they going to meet
4 Are the children going to have

C

1 are going   2 to sleep   3 are
4 is going   5 are not going
6 isn't   7 Are you going   8 Are   9 going

D

1 am going to be
2 is going to take care of
3 aren't[are not] going to play
4 Are you going to wear

UNIT 08   Can, May
Can, May

p.18-19

A

1 see   2 be   3 can call   4 go   5 Can
6 can   7 cannot   8 I read   9 may not leave

B

1 허가   2 추측   3 허가   4 능력   5 능력
6 허가   7 요청   8 추측   9 능력

C

1 May I borrow   2 Can you spell
3 May I turn on

D

1 Can you draw   2 may move
3 Can[May] I eat   4 can't[may not] bring

UNIT 09   Should, Must, Have to
Should, Must, Have to

p.20-21

A

1 shouldn't eat   2 shouldn't play
3 should stay   4 should see   5 should go
6 shouldn't believe   7 should get
8 should be   9 should study

B

1 must arrive   2 must not cross
3 must not smoke   4 must not forget
5 must wear   6 must not swim
7 must take   8 must be, must not make

C

1 have to   2 has to   3 don't have to
4 has to   5 doesn't have to   6 have to
7 don't have to

D

1 Should I help her?
2 You must not drink this water.
3 Do we have to finish this
4 Natalie doesn't have to take the test.

UNIT 10   의문사 1
Interrogatives 1

p.22-23

A

1 What   2 What   3 What   4 Who
5 Whose   6 Whom   7 Which   8 Whose
9 Which

B

1 Whose   2 What   3 Which   4 Who
5 What   6 Which   7 Whose

C

1 Whose turn   2 Who can speak
3 Who(m) will you   4 Which do you

D

1 Who(m) did you invite   2 What food
3 Which room   4 Whose lunchbox

UNIT 11   의문사 2
Interrogatives 2

p.24-25

A

1 Where   2 How   3 Why   4 Where
5 When   6 Why   7 How   8 much   9 far

B

1 How long 2 How 3 How far
4 How old 5 How many 6 How much
7 How often

C

1 Where did you 2 Why are you
3 How do they 4 How, often does he

D

1 Where was he
2 How did they get
3 What time do you get up
4 How many days

UNIT 12 비교급
Comparatives

p.26-27

A

1 darker 2 fatter 3 larger 4 richer
5 busier 6 higher 7 thinner
8 more delicious 9 worse 10 less
11 more 12 lazier 13 more important
14 cleaner 15 warmer 16 happier
17 more famous 18 safer 19 prettier

B

1 more expensive than 2 faster than
3 heavier than 4 more beautiful than
5 hotter than 6 sweeter than
7 more careful than 8 brighter than
9 more dangerous than

C

1 easier 2 more tired 3 older 4 better
5 more 6 less 7 earlier 8 mine
9 much

D

1 bigger than 2 more difficult than
3 more slowly 4 worse than

UNIT 13 최상급
Superlatives

p.28-29

A

1 softest 2 saddest 3 deepest
4 easiest 5 strongest 6 most difficult
7 cheapest 8 most beautiful
9 fattest 10 hottest
11 most interesting 12 largest
13 most expensive 14 happiest
15 smallest 16 best 17 worst
18 most 19 least

B

1 the richest 2 the heaviest
3 the smallest 4 the most famous
5 the wisest 6 the most expensive
7 the prettiest 8 the most dangerous
9 the highest

C

1 darker 2 higher 3 worst 4 laziest
5 funnier 6 best 7 sharper 8 most
9 most diligent

D

1 the best 2 the hottest
3 the slowest 4 the most serious

UNIT 14 명령문, 제안문
Imperatives, Suggestions

p.30-31

A

1 Feed 2 Be 3 Don't 4 not run
5 sing 6 not 7 not play 8 meet 9 or

B

1 Please don't do that again.
2 Don't be shy.
3 Let's not take a walk.
4 Let's not change our plans.

C

1 go 2 say 3 walk 4 Be 5 look

D

1 be 2 don't make 3 Let's buy

4 Let's not wake

UNIT 15 감탄문, 부가 의문문
Exclamations, Tag Questions

p.32-33

A

1 How 2 What 3 How 4 What 5 How

6 What 7 How 8 How 9 What

B

1 How well Andy paints!

2 How handsome the actor is!

3 What an old house it is!

4 What happy children they are!

C

1 is it 2 doesn't he 3 aren't they

4 are we 5 didn't you 6 does she

7 can't she 8 will you 9 shall we

D

1 What a sad story

2 How well

3 was boring, wasn't it

4 don't live here, do they

MEMO

MEMO

MEMO

MEMO

MEMO

MEMO

MEMO

Grammar
Mate 2

Your Best Friend on the Way to Becoming a Grammar Master

Grammar
Mate 2

WORKBOOK

DARAKWON

Grammar Mate 2

WORKBOOK

Contents

01 현재진행형 Present Continuous

A ( ) 안의 말을 이용하여 현재진행형 문장을 완성하세요.

0   I _____am going_____ home now. (go)

1   The cat _____ in the box. (sleep)

2   He _____ his homework. (not, do)

3   The singer _____ at the moment. (not, sing)

4   Lucy _____ a red scarf. (wear)

5   The two men _____ hands. (shake)

6   William _____ his hands. (not, wash)

7   The boy _____ the pasta. (not, eat)

8   Kelly and I _____ in the library. (study)

9   You _____ on the chair. (not, sit)

B 보기에서 알맞은 말을 골라 현재진행형으로 바꾸어 대화를 완성하세요.

보기	lie	~~ring~~	snow	swim

0   A: _____Is_____ the fire alarm _____ringing_____?

B: Yes, it is.

1   A: _____ you _____ on the sofa?

B: No, I'm not.

2   A: _____ the children _____ in the pool?

B: Yes, they are.

3   A: _____ it _____ outside now?

B: No, it isn't.

C 밑줄 친 부분을 바르게 고치세요.

0   I <u>listening</u> to music now.   →   am listening

1   Dad is <u>shaveing</u> his mustache.   →

2   Sue is <u>cuting</u> a pineapple.   →

3   The dog is <u>runing</u> after the squirrel.   →

4   They aren't <u>speak</u> English.   →

5   He <u>not is</u> wearing a cap.   →

6   My friend and I <u>am</u> drinking cocoa.   →

7   <u>They are</u> playing in the garden?   →

8   Is your brother <u>read</u> a book?   →

9   <u>Is</u> Sean and Sally riding their bicycles?   →

D ( ) 안의 말을 이용하여 우리말을 영어로 옮기세요.

0   그들은 지도를 보고 있다. (look)

    → They _____are looking_____ at the map.

1   너는 버스를 기다리고 있니? (wait)

    → _____ for a bus?

2   그 남자는 머리를 자르고 있다. (get)

    → The man _____ a haircut.

3   그 식물들은 죽어가고 있다. (die)

    → The plants _____ .

4   그 학생은 수업에 집중하고 있지 않다. (pay)

    → The student _____ attention in class.

A ( ) 안에서 알맞은 말을 골라 문장을 완성하세요.

0 (now, every day)

   (1) Julie is exercising _____*now*_____.

   (2) Kevin walks his dog _____*every day*_____.

1 (right now, once a month)

   (1) We are taking a test _____.

   (2) They go fishing _____.

2 (at the moment, often)

   (1) I _____ eat cereal for breakfast.

   (2) Tracy is driving _____.

B ( ) 안의 말을 이용하여 현재형 또는 현재진행형 문장을 완성하세요.

0 They _____*are watching*_____ a cartoon now. (watch)

1 I _____ for two hours every day. (study)

2 The boy _____ with his toy trains now. (play)

3 Paul _____ up early in the morning. (get)

4 In Mexico, people _____ Spanish. (speak)

5 The cat _____ its food now. (eat)

6 Chris _____ two sisters. (have)

7 Fred and Sue _____ their puppies. (love)

8 They _____ a roller coaster now. (ride)

9 Sophia often _____ sneakers. (wear)

C ( ) 안에서 알맞은 말을 고르세요.

0   Ann (is | does) going to an English academy.

1   I (am not, don't) remember my mom's phone number.

2   (Are, Do) you understand pop songs?

3   Tom (isn't, doesn't) washing his face.

4   (Is, Does) it always snow in Alaska?

5   My brother (isn't, doesn't) have a job at the moment.

6   Jake, (are, do) you listening to me?

7   Kelly and Philip are (run, running) together.

8   Rabbits (are not, don't) eat meat.

9   Daniel (isn't, doesn't) cooking in the kitchen now.

D ( ) 안의 말을 이용하여 우리말을 영어로 옮기세요.

0   나는 숲 속에서 걷고 있다. (walk)

→ I _____ *am walking* _____ in the forest.

1   Ben은 새 이어폰을 원한다. (want)

→ Ben _____ new earphones.

2   너는 네 방을 청소하고 있니? (clean)

→ _____ your room?

3   그는 그 의자를 사용하고 있지 않다. (use)

→ He _____ the chair.

4   그들은 즐거운 시간을 보내고 있다. (have)

→ They _____ a good time.

03 Be동사의 과거형 Past Simple: *Be*

A ( ) 안에서 알맞은 말을 고르세요.

0 I ((was,) were) very tired last night.

1 The book (wasn't, weren't) interesting.

2 We (was, were) in Sydney last winter.

3 Bill (wasn't, weren't) at home an hour ago.

4 (Was, Were) you sick yesterday?

5 The car keys (was, were) not in my pocket.

6 Ben and Jane (was, were) at the beach yesterday.

7 The new cellphone (was, were) too expensive.

8 (Was, Were) it a nice trip?

9 They (wasn't, weren't) at the party last night.

B ( ) 안의 말과 be동사를 이용하여 과거형 의문문과 대답을 완성하세요.

0 A: _____Was he_____ your best friend? (he)

   B: Yes, _____he was_____.

1 A: _____ in Busan last week? (they)

   B: No, _____.

2 A: _____ a good student? (you)

   B: Yes, _____.

3 A: _____ a nurse? (your mother)

   B: Yes, _____.

4 A: _____ delicious? (the food)

   B: No, _____.

C 보기에서 알맞은 말을 골라 문장을 완성하세요. (중복 가능)

보기	am	is	are	was	were

0   I _____am_____ 16 years old this year.

1   It _____ very cold last winter.

2   Fresh fruits and vegetables _____ good for you.

3   _____ you busy last weekend?

4   _____ Mark at school now?

5   Shakespeare _____ a great writer.

6   I _____ in New York two months ago.

7   Egypt _____ not a city.

D ( ) 안의 말을 이용하여 우리말을 영어로 옮기세요.

0   그 웨이터는 불친절했다. (the waiter)

   →   _____The waiter was_____ unkind.

1   그 달걀들은 신선하지 않았다. (the eggs)

   →   _____ fresh.

2   수학 시험은 어려웠니? (the math test)

   →   _____ difficult?

3   너는 서울에서 태어났니? (you)

   →   _____ born in Seoul?

4   우리는 지난 주말에 집에 있지 않았다. (we)

   →   _____ at home last weekend.

A 주어진 동사의 과거형을 쓰세요.

0	wash	–	washed		
1	help	–			
2	close	–			
3	arrive	–			
4	study	–			
5	try	–			
6	play	–			
7	stop	–			
8	drop	–			
9	plan	–			

10	come	–
11	build	–
12	catch	–
13	do	–
14	eat	–
15	hear	–
16	leave	–
17	make	–
18	run	–
19	write	–

B 주어진 동사의 현재형 또는 과거형을 써서 문장을 완성하세요.

0   walk   (1) He ____walks____ to school every day.

               (2) He ____walked____ to school yesterday.

1   cry   (1) Babies _____.

               (2) The baby _____ last night.

2   go   (1) We _____ swimming in summer.

               (2) We _____ swimming last Sunday.

3   meet   (1) I _____ her every day.

               (2) I _____ her every day last week.

4   read   (1) The boy _____ a lot of books.

               (2) The boy _____ the book two days ago.

C ( ) 안의 말을 이용하여 과거형 문장을 완성하세요.

0   I _____cut_____ my finger by mistake. (cut)

1   Emily _____ her mom after school. (call)

2   I _____ only two meals yesterday. (eat)

3   My brother and I _____ the table for dinner. (set)

4   Mr. Lee _____ our class last year. (teach)

5   Peter _____ a new car two weeks ago. (buy)

6   The children _____ in the river. (swim)

7   My boyfriend _____ my backpack for me. (carry)

8   We _____ kangaroos at the zoo. (see)

9   Jane _____ the difficult test yesterday. (pass)

D ( ) 안의 말을 이용하여 우리말을 영어로 옮기세요.

0   Eric은 일등상을 탔다. (win)

　　→ Eric _____won_____ first prize.

1   나는 3년 전에 파리에서 살았다. (live)

　　→ I _____ in Paris three years ago.

2   우리는 어제 해변에 차를 몰고 갔다. (drive)

　　→ We _____ to the beach yesterday.

3   그 아이들은 빨간 신호등에서 멈췄다. (stop)

　　→ The children _____ at the red light.

4   나는 나의 엄마를 위해 카드를 만들었다. (make)

　　→ I _____ a card for my mom.

일반동사의 과거형 2 Past Simple 2

A ( ) 안의 말을 이용하여 과거형 부정문을 완성하세요. (줄임말을 쓸 것)

0   We _____ didn't go _____ out last weekend. (go)

1   Sara _____ a doctor yesterday. (see)

2   Sorry. I _____ your name. (hear)

3   They _____ anything today. (eat)

4   His car _____ this morning. (start)

5   She _____ well last night. (sleep)

6   Five students _____ their homework. (do)

7   Karen _____ her jacket. (bring)

8   My dad _____ early tonight. (come)

9   The train _____ on time. (leave)

B ( ) 안의 말을 이용하여 과거형 의문문과 대답을 완성하세요.

0   A: _____ Did _____ Mike _____ cut _____ the grass yesterday? (cut)

   B: Yes, _____ he did _____.

1   A: _____ something _____ off the table? (fall)

   B: No, _____.

2   A: _____ she _____ her student ID card? (lose)

   B: Yes, _____.

3   A: _____ the boy _____ a letter to Santa? (send)

   B: Yes, _____.

4   A: _____ your parents _____ on vacation last week? (go)

   B: No, _____.

C 주어진 문장을 ( ) 안의 지시대로 바꿔 쓰세요.

0 We had homework yesterday. (부정문)

→ _____We didn't have homework yesterday._____

1 She called 119 this morning. (의문문)

→ _____

2 I met my friend last weekend. (부정문)

→ _____

3 They studied for a test last week. (의문문)

→ _____

4 You washed the dishes after dinner. (부정문)

→ _____

D ( ) 안의 말을 이용하여 우리말을 영어로 옮기세요.

0 우리 엄마는 가스를 잠그지 않았다. (turn off)

→ My mom _____didn't turn off_____ the gas.

1 우리는 택시를 타지 않았다. (take)

→ We _____ a taxi.

2 너는 네 점심을 가져왔니? (bring)

→ _____ your lunch?

3 Amy와 Ted는 그 동아리에 가입했니? (join)

→ _____ the club?

4 그 콘서트는 7시에 시작하지 않았다. (start)

→ The concert _____ at 7 o'clock.

06 미래 표현 1: Will Future Time 1: *Will*

A ( ) 안에서 알맞은 말을 고르세요.

0   I (call, (will call)) you tomorrow.

1   In five years, Julie (is, will be) a university student.

2   (Are, Will) you watch a movie tonight?

3   Sam will (go, goes) to France this summer.

4   Will they (are, be) here on Monday?

5   We will (have, having) a test next week.

6   I am sorry. I (am not, won't) be late again.

7   Will (they finish, finish they) their work soon?

8   Will the plane (arrive, arrives) at 5 o'clock?

9   Don't drink that milk. You (get, will get) sick.

B will과 ( ) 안의 말을 이용하여 문장을 완성하세요.

0   My uncle _____will open_____ a restaurant next month. (open)

1   Peter _____ for Busan on Friday. (leave)

2   It _____ rainy this evening. (not, be)

3   We _____ on a picnic this weekend. (not, go)

4   _____ you _____ Jim to the party? (invite)

5   Susan _____ in London for a year. (work)

6   I _____ those jeans. (not, buy)

7   My father _____ me. (not, forgive)

8   _____ you _____ famous in the future? (be)

9   _____ Peter _____ the soccer team? (join)

C 보기에서 알맞은 말을 골라 will과 함께 써서 대화를 완성하세요. (단, 한 번씩만 쓸 것)

보기	buy	~~carry~~	do	make

0 A: These books are so heavy.

B: Don't worry. I _____will carry_____ them for you.

1 A: I'm really hungry.

B: I _____ some sandwiches.

2 A: Jake, did you finish your homework?

B: No, I didn't. I _____ it later.

3 A: We don't have any milk.

B: Really? I _____ some now.

D will과 ( ) 안의 말을 이용하여 우리말을 영어로 옮기세요.

0 수업은 5분 후에 시작할 것이다. (start)

→ The class _____will start_____ in five minutes.

1 내가 전화를 받을게. (answer)

→ I _____ the phone.

2 우리는 그 콘서트에 가지 않을 것이다. (go)

→ We _____ to the concert.

3 나는 미래에 수의사가 될 것이다. (be)

→ I _____ a vet in the future.

4 그들이 시험에 합격할까? (pass)

→ _____ the exam?

07 미래 표현 2: Be going to Future Time 2: *Be going to*

A 보기에서 알맞은 말을 골라 be going to와 함께 써서 문장을 완성하세요

| 보기 | buy | call | find | go | skip | stay | ~~snow~~ | wear |

0   The weather is cold. It _____*is going to snow*_____.

1   Jack has a job interview. He _____ a suit.

2   I am not hungry. I _____ lunch.

3   It's far to the airport. Susan _____ a taxi.

4   We _____ to the magic show. We have the tickets.

5   John _____ a new car. He is saving money.

6   I'm not going to go out tonight. I _____ at home.

7   Mary doesn't like her job. She _____ a better job.

B ( ) 안의 말을 알맞게 배열하여 문장을 완성하세요.

0   (the bus, arrive, is, going, to)

→ _____*The bus is going to arrive*_____ soon.

1   (going, their, to, is, be, new album)

→ _____ very popular.

2   (are, to, going, not, go, we)

→ _____ to Busan.

3   (they, to, going, meet, are)

→ _____ at 7 o'clock?

4   (going, have, to, the children, are)

→ _____ lunch?

C 밑줄 친 부분을 바르게 고치세요.

0   Rick is going to <u>buying</u> a new guitar.   →   buy

1   We <u>going</u> to play soccer tomorrow.   →

2   I'm going <u>sleep</u> at my friend's house tonight. →

3   We <u>will</u> going to go hiking next weekend.   →

4   It <u>goes</u> to rain tomorrow.   →

5   They <u>are going not</u> to visit us next week.   →

6   He <u>won't</u> going to sing at the festival.   →

7   <u>Do you going</u> to read the book?   →

8   <u>Is</u> Joe and Sue going to be late?   →

9   Are they <u>go</u> to take a walk after lunch?   →

D be going to와 ( ) 안의 말을 이용하여 우리말을 영어로 옮기세요.

0   그는 내일 아침 일찍 집을 떠날 것이다. (leave)

→ He _____is going to leave_____ home early tomorrow morning.

1   나는 내년에 17살이 될 것이다. (be)

→ I _____ 17 years old next year.

2   Sally는 방과 후에 그녀의 남동생을 돌볼 것이다. (take care of)

→ Sally _____ her brother after school.

3   우리는 다음 주에 농구를 하지 않을 것이다. (play)

→ We _____ basketball next week.

4   너는 오늘밤에 저 드레스를 입을 거니? (wear)

→ _____ that dress tonight?

08 **Can, May** *Can, May*

A ( ) 안에서 알맞은 말을 고르세요.

0   Rosa can (speak, speaks) Italian.

1   Cats can (see, seeing) well at night.

2   They may (are, be) at home now.

3   You (call can, can call) me anytime tomorrow.

4   He may (go, going) to Boston next year.

5   (Can, May) you hear me right now?

6   Stella (cans, can) type really fast.

7   My brother (cannot, doesn't can) drive a car.

8   May (I read, read I) this magazine?

9   You (may not leave, may leave not) now.

B 밑줄 친 부분의 의미로 알맞은 것을 고르세요.

0   Brian isn't in class today. He <u>may</u> be sick.   ☑ 추측   ☐ 허가

1   <u>Can</u> I go to the restroom?   ☐ 능력   ☐ 허가

2   The woman <u>may</u> be over fifty.   ☐ 추측   ☐ 허가

3   You <u>may</u> play with my toys.   ☐ 추측   ☐ 허가

4   Nick is tall. He <u>can</u> reach the top shelf.   ☐ 능력   ☐ 허가

5   I <u>can't</u> open the door. My hands are full.   ☐ 능력   ☐ 허가

6   <u>May</u> I try on these pants?   ☐ 추측   ☐ 허가

7   <u>Can</u> you keep this secret?   ☐ 허가   ☐ 요청

8   Hurry up. You <u>may</u> miss the bus.   ☐ 추측   ☐ 허가

9   This watch is too expensive. I <u>can't</u> buy it.   ☐ 능력   ☐ 요청

C 보기에서 알맞은 말을 골라 ( ) 안의 말과 함께 써서 대화를 완성하세요. (단, 한 번씩만 쓸 것)

보기	borrow	~~open~~	spell	turn on

0 A: It's hot in here. _____*Can you open*_____ the window? (can)

B: Of course. I'd be happy to.

1 A: _____ your pen? (may)

B: Sorry. I'm using it right now.

2 A: _____ your name? (can)

B: Sure. My name is M-I-C-H-A-E-L.

3 A: _____ the TV? (may)

B: No problem. The remote control is on the table.

D ( ) 안의 말을 이용하여 우리말을 영어로 옮기세요.

0 Sujin은 프랑스어로 된 책을 읽을 수 있다. (read)

→ Sujin _____*can read*_____ a book in Franch.

1 너는 기린을 그릴 수 있니? (draw)

→ _____ a giraffe?

2 우리는 내년에 제주도로 이사를 갈지도 모른다. (move)

→ We _____ to Jejudo next year.

3 이 케이크를 먹어도 될까요? (eat)

→ _____ this cake?

4 너는 여기에 음식을 가져와서는 안 된다. (bring)

→ You _____ your food here.

Should, Must, Have to *Should, Must, Have to*

A should/shouldn't와 ( ) 안의 말을 함께 써서 문장을 완성하세요.

0   You look tired. You _____should get_____ some rest. (get)

1   Mike is getting fat. He _____ more fast food. (eat)

2   He _____ the music too loudly at night. (play)

3   Sarah is lonely. We _____ with her. (stay)

4   You _____ that movie. It's great! (see)

5   It's 10 o'clock. The kids _____ to bed now. (go)

6   She _____ him. He's a big liar. (believe)

7   Kevin watches TV all day. He _____ some exercise. (get)

8   The boy is often rude. He _____ more polite. (be)

9   The final exam is next week. We _____ for it now. (study)

B must/must not과 ( ) 안의 말을 함께 써서 문장을 완성하세요.

0   It's too late. I _____must go_____ home now. (go)

1   They _____ at work before 8:30. (arrive)

2   You _____ the road now. The traffic light is red. (cross)

3   Passengers _____ on the plane. (smoke)

4   Kevin _____ his homework again. (forget)

5   Students _____ their name tags at school. (wear)

6   You _____ in this river. It is very deep. (swim)

7   The mother kangaroo _____ care of her baby kangaroo. (take)

8   You _____ quiet in the library. You _____ any noise. (be, make)

C 보기에서 알맞은 말을 골라 문장을 완성하세요. (중복 가능)

보기	have to	has to	don't have to	doesn't have to

0   The food is free. You _____don't have to_____ pay for it.

1   We _____ hurry. We don't have much time now.

2   Kevin _____ change his clothes. They are wet.

3   It's very warm today. I _____ wear my jacket.

4   Ann _____ take the bus to school. It's far from her house.

5   David wears a uniform at work. He _____ buy many clothes.

6   Does he _____ wear glasses to read?

7   I _____ clean my room. I cleaned it today.

D 우리말과 일치하도록 ( ) 안의 말을 알맞게 배열하세요.

0   우리는 7시 전에 공항에 도착해야 한다. (must, we, arrive, the airport, at)

→ _____We must arrive at the airport_____ before 7 o'clock.

1   내가 그녀를 도와주어야 할까? (help, I, should, her)

→ _____

2   너는 이 물을 마시면 안 된다. (drink, not, you, must, water, this)

→ _____

3   우리가 오늘 이것을 끝내야 하니? (have, to, this, we, finish, do)

→ _____ today?

4   Natalie는 그 시험을 볼 필요가 없다. (doesn't, to, take, Natalie, have, the test)

→ _____

A ( ) 안에서 알맞은 말을 고르세요.

0 ((Who,) What) is your teacher?

1 (Who, What) is your mother's name?

2 (What, Which) do they grow in their garden?

3 (What, Whom) is your hobby?

4 (Who, Whom) fixed the bicycle for you?

5 (Whom, Whose) father is he?

6 (What, Whom) did you call last night?

7 (Which, What) day should we go, Monday or Tuesday?

8 (Who, Whose) dictionary is on the table?

9 (Which, What) team won the game, the L.A. Dodgers or the Chicago Cubs?

B 보기에서 알맞은 말을 골라 대화를 완성하세요. (중복 가능)

보기	who	whose	what	which

0 A: _____Who_____ did Romeo love?   B: He loved Juliet.

1 A: _____ teddy bear is this?   B: It's my sister's.

2 A: _____ does your father do?   B: He is a teacher.

3 A: _____ is better, this one or that one? B: That one.

4 A: _____ invented the light bulb?   B: Thomas Edison.

5 A: _____ are they looking at?   B: They are looking at birds.

6 A: _____ bag is yours?   B: The blue one.

7 A: _____ cellphone is this?   B: It's mine.

C 밑줄 친 부분을 묻는 의문문이 되도록 빈칸에 알맞은 말을 쓰세요.

0 A: ___What___ ___did___ Alex buy?

B: He bought a new pair of shoes.

1 A: _____ _____ is it?

B: It is my turn.

2 A: _____ _____ _____ English here?

B: David can speak English.

3 A: _____ _____ _____ visit in L.A.?

B: I will visit my cousin.

4 A: _____ _____ _____ like better, apples or pears?

B: I like apples better.

D ( ) 안의 말을 이용하여 우리말을 영어로 옮기세요.

0 누가 너의 가장 친한 친구니? (be)

→ _____Who is_____ your best friend?

1 너는 네 파티에 누구를 초대했니? (invite)

→ _____ to your party?

2 그녀는 어떤 음식을 좋아하니? (food)

→ _____ does she like?

3 어느 방이 네 방이니? (room)

→ _____ is yours?

4 이것은 누구의 도시락이니? (lunchbox)

→ _____ is this?

A ( ) 안에서 알맞은 말을 고르세요.

0   A: ((When) How) is the concert?   B: Tomorrow at 8:00 p.m.

1   A: (Where, How) do you live?   B: I live near Bacon Park.

2   A: (When, How) was your exam?   B: It was difficult.

3   A: (Why, How) do you sing?   B: Because I love music.

4   A: (Where, When) is he from?   B: He is from Thailand.

5   A: (Where, When) do the shops open?   B: From Monday to Saturday.

6   A: (When, Why) did you go to sleep early?   B: Because I was so tired.

7   A: (Why, How) do you go to school?   B: By bus.

8   A: How (many, much) is this jacket?   B: It's only $20.

9   A: How (long, far) is your school from here?   B: It's about 1km.

B 보기에서 알맞은 말을 골라 대화를 완성하세요.

보기	how	how far	how often	how old
	how tall	how long	how many	how much

0   A: _____How tall_____ are you?   B: 163cm.

1   A: _____ will you stay here?   B: For three days.

2   A: _____ did you learn English?   B: I practiced it every day.

3   A: _____ is the post office from here? B: It's a five-minute walk.

4   A: _____ is your father?   B: Fifty-four.

5   A: _____ students are there?   B: About twenty.

6   A: _____ money do we have?   B: $50.

7   A: _____ does he go jogging?   B: Every day.

C 밑줄 친 부분을 묻는 의문문이 되도록 빈칸에 알맞은 말을 쓰세요.

0 A: ___When___ ___is___ your birthday?

 B: My birthday is next week.

1 A: _____ _____ _____ buy that coat?

 B: I bought it at the store near my house.

2 A: _____ _____ _____ running?

 B: I'm running because I am late.

3 A: _____ _____ _____ go to work?

 B: They go to work by subway.

4 A: _____ _____ _____ _____ go to the gym?

 B: He goes to the gym twice a week.

D ( ) 안의 말을 이용하여 우리말을 영어로 옮기세요.

0 너는 왜 영어를 공부하니? (study)

 → _____Why do you study_____ English?

1 그는 어젯밤에 어디에 있었니? (be)

 → _____ last night?

2 그들은 공항까지 어떻게 갔니? (get)

 → _____ to the airport?

3 너는 아침에 몇 시에 일어나니? (time, get up)

 → _____ in the morning?

4 7월은 며칠이 있니? (day)

 → _____ are there in July?

A 주어진 단어의 비교급을 쓰세요.

0	cold	–	colder	10	little	–	
1	dark	–		11	many	–	
2	fat	–		12	lazy	–	
3	large	–		13	important	–	
4	rich	–		14	clean	–	
5	busy	–		15	warm	–	
6	high	–		16	happy	–	
7	thin	–		17	famous	–	
8	delicious	–		18	safe	–	
9	bad	–		19	pretty	–	

B ( ) 안의 말을 이용하여 비교급 문장을 완성하세요.

0 My hair is _____longer than_____ Kate's. (long)

1 The jacket is _____ the skirt. (expensive)

2 A jet is _____ a helicopter. (fast)

3 My bag is _____ yours. (heavy)

4 Kelly is _____ her sisters. (beautiful)

5 This summer is _____ last summer. (hot)

6 The red apple is _____ the green apple. (sweet)

7 Eric is _____ Mike. (careful)

8 This lamp is _____ that one. (bright)

9 A motorcycle is _____ a bicycle. (dangerous)

C ( ) 안에서 알맞은 말을 고르세요.

0   John is (taller, more taller) than Mike.

1   English is (easy, easier) than science.

2   I am (tired, more tired) than you are.

3   Who is (old, older), you or Emily?

4   My English is (gooder, better) than my Spanish.

5   I have (many, more) pencils than you.

6   Bob makes (little, less) money than Steve.

7   I came home (earlier, more early) than my sister.

8   Grandpa's glasses are thicker than (me, mine).

9   The ocean is (very, much) deeper than the river.

D ( ) 안의 말을 이용하여 우리말을 영어로 옮기세요.

0   Ashley는 Olivia보다 더 열심히 공부한다. (hard)

→ Ashley studies _____harder than_____ Olivia.

1   내 형의 방은 내 방보다 더 크다. (big)

→ My brother's room is _____ my room.

2   이번 시험은 지난 시험보다 더 어려웠다. (difficult)

→ This test was _____ the last one.

3   더 천천히 말씀해주시겠습니까? (slowly)

→ Could you speak _____?

4   내 점수는 네 점수보다 더 나쁘다. (bad)

→ My score is _____ your score.

13 최상급 Superlatives

A 주어진 단어의 최상급을 쓰세요.

0	nice	–	nicest	10	hot	–	
1	soft	–		11	interesting	–	
2	sad	–		12	large	–	
3	deep	–		13	expensive	–	
4	easy	–		14	happy	–	
5	strong	–		15	small	–	
6	difficult	–		16	good	–	
7	cheap	–		17	bad	–	
8	beautiful	–		18	many	–	
9	fat	–		19	little	–	

B ( ) 안의 말을 이용하여 최상급 문장을 완성하세요.

0   Sophia is _____the youngest_____ person in her family. (young)

1   Who is _____ man in the world? (rich)

2   The red box is _____ of the three. (heavy)

3   My bedroom is _____ room in my house. (small)

4   She is _____ actress in the country. (famous)

5   He is _____ person in this town. (wise)

6   The woman bought _____ bag in the shop. (expensive)

7   This is _____ dress of them all. (pretty)

8   Sharks are _____ animals in the sea. (dangerous)

9   Mt. Everest is _____ mountain in the world. (high)

C ( ) 안에서 알맞은 말을 고르세요.

0 Joshua is the (fast, faster, (fastest)) runner in the class.

1 Her skin is (dark, darker, darkest) than my skin.

2 An airplane flies (high, higher, highest) than a bird.

3 He was the (worse, baddest, worst) singer of all.

4 My brother is the (lazier, laziest, most lazy) person in my family.

5 My uncle is (funny, funnier, the funniest) than my dad.

6 This is the (goodest, most good, best) song on this album.

7 The knife is (sharp, sharper, sharpest) than the scissors.

8 Nick reads the (many, more, most) books of the three.

9 She is the (diligent, diligentest, most diligent) girl in the class.

D ( ) 안의 말을 이용하여 우리말을 영어로 옮기세요.

0 Jack은 그 학교에서 가장 인기 있는 소년이다. (popular)

→ Jack is ___the most popular___ boy in the school.

1 세계 최고의 축구 선수는 누구니? (good)

→ Who is _____ soccer player in the world?

2 오늘은 1년 중 가장 더운 날이다. (hot)

→ Today is _____ day of the year.

3 나무늘보는 세계에서 가장 느린 동물이다. (slow)

→ The sloth is _____ animal in the world.

4 대기 오염은 그 나라에서 가장 심각한 문제이다. (serious)

→ Air pollution is _____ problem in the country.

명령문, 제안문 Imperatives, Suggestions

A ( ) 안에서 알맞은 말을 고르세요.

0 Please ((clean,) cleans) your room.

1 (Feed, Feeding) the dog at 5 o'clock.

2 (Be, Do) nice to your friends.

3 (Don't, Not) open the window.

4 Do (run not, not run) in the classroom.

5 Let's (sing, singing) together.

6 Let's (don't, not) talk about it now.

7 Let's (play not, not play) soccer today.

8 Why don't we (meet, meeting) on Monday?

9 Hurry up, (and, or) you will miss the show!

B 주어진 문장을 부정문으로 바꿔 쓰세요.

0 Close your book.

→ _____ Don't close your book. _____

1 Please do that again.

→ _____

2 Be shy.

→ _____

3 Let's take a walk.

→ _____

4 Let's change our plans.

→ _____

C 보기에서 알맞은 말을 골라 문장을 완성하세요. (단, 한 번씩만 쓸 것)

> 보기 ~~do~~   go   say

0 _____Do_____ your homework now.

1 Let's not _____ out. It's too cold.

2 I didn't hear you. Please _____ that again.

> 보기 be   look   walk

3 Let's _____. It's not far from here.

4 _____ a good student.

5 A: What's the date today?

B: I don't know. Let's _____ at the calendar.

D ( ) 안의 말을 이용하여 우리말을 영어로 옮기세요.

0 가족들과 즐거운 시간 보내. (have)

→ _____Have_____ a good time with your family.

1 항상 정직해라. (be)

→ Always _____ honest.

2 제발 떠들지 마세요. (make)

→ Please _____ any noise.

3 영화 시작 전에 팝콘을 좀 사자. (buy)

→ _____ some popcorn before the movie.

4 그를 깨우지 말자. (wake)

→ _____ him up.

15 감탄문, 부가 의문문 Exclamations, Tag Questions

A ( ) 안에서 알맞은 말을 고르세요.

0   ((What,) How) a great idea it is!

1   (What, How) cute the puppy is!

2   (What, How) a wonderful view it is!

3   (What, How) difficult the math test was!

4   (What, How) nice shoes they are!

5   (What, How) funny the movie was!

6   (What, How) a lovely garden they have!

7   (What, How) fast he is running!

8   (What, How) delicious this cake is!

9   (What, How) a delicious meal it was!

B 다음 문장을 ( ) 안의 말로 시작하는 감탄문으로 바꿔 쓰세요.

0   It is very cold today. (how)

→ _____ How cold it is today! _____

1   Andy paints very well. (how)

→ _____

2   The actor is very handsome. (how)

→ _____

3   It is a very old house! (what)

→ _____

4   They are very happy children. (what)

→ _____

C 빈칸에 알맞은 부가 의문문을 써서 문장을 완성하세요.

0   She is your mother, _____ *isn't she* _____?

1   This isn't very interesting, _____?

2   Mr. Kim teaches music, _____?

3   Pat and Joe are from Brazil, _____?

4   We are not late, _____?

5   You bought the tickets, _____?

6   She doesn't like spicy food, _____?

7   Your sister can speak French, _____?

8   Open the window, _____?

9   Let's go to the zoo, _____?

D ( ) 안의 말을 이용하여 우리말을 영어로 옮기세요.

0   그 아기는 정말 사랑스럽구나! (lovely)

→ _____ *How lovely* _____ the baby is!

1   그것은 정말 슬픈 이야기구나! (a sad story)

→ _____ it is!

2   그녀는 노래를 정말 잘 하는구나! (well)

→ _____ she sings!

3   그 연극은 지루했어, 그렇지 않니? (boring)

→ The play _____, _____?

4   그들은 여기에 살지 않아, 그렇지? (live, here)

→ They _____, _____?

MEMO

MEMO

MEMO

MEMO

Grammar Mate 2

Grammar Mate is a three-level grammar series for intermediate learners. This series is designed to help students understand basic English grammar with various step-by-step exercises. All chapters offer writing exercises to strengthen students' writing abilities and grammatical accuracy as well as review tests to prepare them for actual school tests. This series can be used by teachers in the classroom, by tutors teaching a small group of students, and by students for self-study purposes. With this series, students will improve their confidence in English. In addition, they will develop a solid foundation in English grammar to prepare themselves for a more advanced level.

Key Features

- Core basic English grammar
- Easy, clear explanations of grammar rules and concepts
- Plenty of various step-by-step exercises
- Writing exercises to develop writing skills and grammatical accuracy
- Comprehensive tests to prepare for actual school tests
- Workbook for further practice

Components Student Book | Workbook | Answer Key

Online Resources : www.darakwon.co.kr

Vocabulary Lists & Tests | Sentence Lists & Tests | Extra Exercises | Midterm & Final Exams

Grammar Mate Series

QR코드를 통해 본 교재의 상세 정보 및
부가학습 자료를 이용하실 수 있습니다.